Contents

Acknowledgments

I would like to take this time to thank some very special people who were instrumental in my life and gave me the inspiration to write this book.

First would be my father, Dominic "Doc" Scala. They called him "Doc" because he worked as a longshoreman "on the docks"—the Brooklyn piers. He was the one who introduced me to the game that I learned to love. A pretty fair athlete in his own right, he was an amateur boxing champion in the Golden Gloves middleweight division. He always had time to take me to the park and play ball. He was also a master at getting the local sportswriter to come to the games and write about me. The funny part is I always gave them something good to write about after the game was over.

To this day I well up when I think of all my mom put up with in our Brooklyn household. She was the glue that held the family together. I think of her constantly washing baseball, basketball, and football uniforms. I think of her tending to my injuries, cleaning cuts and bruises that I couldn't get to. And cooking great food and, of course, serving me wherever I wanted to eat it.

They are both gone now, but their memory will always be with me. God bless you both, and I will always be thankful for the way you guided me.

To George Steinbrenner and the New York Yankees organization for being the family that they are and making me part of that family for nine straight years. I learned so much from so many legends and use that knowledge today in teaching my kids. Being a Yankee is forever, in any capacity on the field. Hell, even Whitey Ford sees me and calls me "Coach." Now, that's a compliment.

To my daughter, Shana, who just graduated from New York University. She is such a joy: smart, beautiful, and independent. She knows what she wants in life, and I have no doubt that she will be a great success. Her passion for life comes out when she does things for people. Thank you, Shana, for making me strive for the next level.

I would like to say a special thanks to my mother-in-law and father-in-law, Lucyann and Joe Cimino. They were always there for me and rooted me on. Oh, and they always bragged about their son-in-law who was a New York Yankee.

To my sisters-in-law Joann, Toni, and Susan, whom I have known for more than 35 years and are more like my sisters.

And, last but not least, to my wife and life partner, Yolanda. She has been there through the good times and bad: Picking me up at the airport at 3 A.M. from a road trip with the Yankees. Coming to Modesto, California, to watch me play in the minor leagues. The sleepless nights when I was sick. The birth of our child. The day she found our first house and brought me in and I looked and said, "Are you kidding me?" She always had vision. Then there was the day she designed a gold- and diamond-encrusted Yankees logo. That one vision became a business that gave us security for many years.

The one thing that we have and will always have is that love that never dies. We are always there for each other and, most important, we enjoy each other's company. We love spending time together, and I am very proud of that after 35 years of being together. I love you, Yolanda, and I will enjoy spending the rest of my life with you.

Foreword

I've known Dom, it seems like, pretty much forever. After our child-hood days spent playing against each other on Brooklyn's famous Parade Grounds, I met up with him again, joined in pinstripes, when he came to the Yankees in 1978 to work in the bull pen. There was word that there was this new character out there with maybe more than his fair share of knowledge about the game. Catchers are the field generals, they say. So I went to look, and there was my old buddy, Dom. If we hadn't been before, we've been good friends ever since. "To this day," he would say in his familiar Brooklynese.

Dom stayed on with the Yankees, while I played second base. We won the World Series in 1978. Dom was still a young guy, but stuck with the Yanks nine years, coaching out of the bull pen, when we had a host of ex-Yankees helping out, including such catching greats as Elston Howard, Jeff Torborg, and Yogi Berra—not to mention our ill-fated hero Thurman Munson. But Dom stood solid among these giants, and I visited him frequently for advice and a little camara-derie, whether it be around the batting cage, in the clubhouse, or going out to dinner.

He and I are the same age (days apart), and from the Brooklyn neighborhoods, so it was natural we'd become very close friends—"to this day."

It's no surprise to me that Dom has become such a successful baseball coach at Adelphi University and has had so much support for his baseball camps for youth in the summer. Whenever I was in need of advice about the game in general, even times when I was a free agent and left the Yankees for the Dodgers, I knew I could count on Dom.

With that bit of introduction, let me tell you that I have known and worked with Dom for many years, and I can tell you he is second to none in working with kids and teaching them his great knowledge of the game of baseball. He preaches the fundamentals, and over the years he has developed many great drills and simple techniques that get his point across.

But, ultimately, the key is that Dom cares about kids, and you can see that just watching him work with the children at his camps. He's got a number of other professionals working with the players, but Dom stays right in the middle of it, preaching his mantra— "fundamentals, boys, always fundamentals."

—WILLIE RANDOLPH

1

Growing Up with a Dream

When I was five, my dad used to take me across the street to McCarren Park in the Williamsburg section of Brooklyn to play catch and teach me to hit a baseball. He was a longshoreman who went to work in the early morning, worked hard on the docks all day, came home at five, and then played ball with me. I don't remember many things about being five years old, but one of my first memories is sitting on the stoop and waiting for him with my glove and a ball. He always seemed to have time to teach me to play the game. I was still a little guy then, but I think that's when the dream began.

Maybe I ought to take a minute to explain what the dream is. Guys who try to make the big leagues know—if you ask a young kid scraping his way through the minors what he's doing, he'll just say, "You know, chasing the dream," and he expects you to understand that—but maybe it's not so crystal clear to everybody else. It really is as simple as it sounds, but for some guys it is a dream that can come true. Why not chase that dream for as long as you can?

Of course, the dream is what every kid starts out with. He watches a big-league game on TV, and he sees the crowds cheering home runs and great plays. He sees the accolades that a ballplayer gets, the celebrity he has. The kid wants to someday be that guy. He dreams that he can be someone people look up to and say, "There he goes." He dreams of making good money and doing something he loves to do. After all, it's a kids' game. Big-league players are playing a kids' game and making really good money these days. They don't have to punch a time clock or get up at six o'clock in the morning and go catch a bus. No, this is something where you're outdoors, and you're in the spotlight at the same time. People love you, they get to know you. What kid doesn't dream of growing up and making money playing a game? It's a daydream that ends pretty early for most everybody, but that's what makes it special. I grew up with that dream.

The Brooklyn we lived in then, when I was a kid, just as the '60s began, was a different place than it is now. I lived in an Italian neighborhood in Williamsburg. Houses and apartment buildings, anywhere from two to six stories high, crowded the tree-lined streets. Most people lived in apartments with railroad rooms, one right after the other in a row. You had no real privacy; you used a folding screen if you were going to change your clothes, like in the old movies. We had to shower in the kitchen. My dad only put in a shower when I was 10 years old; before that I had to wash in the sink. It was pretty tough, where we grew up.

We owned our own "eight-family" house, though, where our family—me, my sister, Dad, and Mom—lived with seven other families. The people in the house came from all over: they were immigrant families from Ireland, Italy, and Germany. Folks of many different ethnic backgrounds lived in Brooklyn at the time, so in that sense, it wasn't too much different from the way it is today. Our immediate neighborhood was Italian, but across McCarren Park, the neighborhoods were German and Irish, and if you went 10 blocks the other way, it was Puerto Rican people; another 10 blocks, you had Hasidic Jews.

The neighborhood was mixed with small businesses and shops; you didn't have to get in the car to get a loaf of bread or a glass of beer. Just on the corner from our house was the Miami bar. There were corner groceries, ice cream parlors, and a lot of candy stores, like Trotta's and Stevie's Candy Store. Joey Pepe's Ice Cream Parlor was right across the street. You would go up the steps and in the door, past the big plate glass window and the red neon lettering that flashed the store's name, and on the right was a counter with stools, to the left stood red vinyl booths, and next to them was a refrigerator box full of iced soda. Ice would slide off the bottles into your hand, which was especially good on a hot summer day after a game. I was always playing something. My favorite soda was a Manhattan Special. It's espresso in a bottle. You can still get it today. It's made in Greenpoint, in Brooklyn, by the fourth generation of a family that came from Naples, by way of Ellis Island.

At Joey's, I'd go into the store, slide onto a stool, and say to him, "Hey, Joey, can I have a sundae? Would ya put it on my mother's bill?" Every day, I walked six blocks to school at Annunciation, and we'd get lunch at the famous Bamonte's Restaurant; it's a Brooklyn landmark, a real New York Italian place. Typically, I would get a meatball sandwich, and I would say, "Put it on my mother's bill." I would split it and give half to my friend. My mother would go around and pay the bills at the end of the week. Everywhere we would go, she'd pay the bills at the end of the week. That's the way we lived, and you knew everybody.

Next to Joey Pepe's was a triangular park, with benches around the sides where people would go to get a breath of fresh air and sit. I remember that when I was kid, all the teenagers would gather there in the evening, and they would sing a cappella in groups. I was a little boy, and I would sit at my window and watch them across the street as groups from different parts of Brooklyn would compete with each other. They sang songs like "So Much in Love" and "Under the Boardwalk," songs that were popular on the radio. I used to sing a little bit, too, when I got older.

Our parish, Our Lady of Mount Carmel, was and still is famous for the "Festa del Giglio," where they "dance the statue." It's a festival where hundreds of men lift and dance a 65-foot statue and an immense *barca* (a boat in Italian, but it's a float for the festival) through the streets of Williamsburg on Giglio Sunday, with games and food, bands playing, and crowds singing and clapping—all the things that make a summer festival. It's part of the southern Italian culture that honors San Paolino (Saint Paulinus) and the Feast of Our Lady of Mount Carmel.

My mom was a short Italian lady who grew up in the Corona section of Queens. She was the person who always watched out for me, because my father would work, of course, from nine to five, and my mom was home. She was always there for me. Let's say I'd get a bad grade in school. She'd say, "I'm going to tell your father when he gets home. You're not going to be able to go out"—and this, that, and the other thing. And of course, my father would come home, the bell would ring, and I would say, "uh-oh." Maybe she would tell him, and maybe she wouldn't. She kept me on my toes.

Of course, she was always a great cook—putting food on the table seemed an indispensable part of her life. Every Sunday morning, I woke up to the smell of meatballs, sausage, and gravy (in an Italian home, "gravy" is a tomato sauce with meat that spends half a day on the stove, best enjoyed by dipping a ripped-off piece of bread into the pot when no one is looking). My father would go out and get a couple of loaves of Italian bread, and that's what I would have for breakfast: a fabulous meatball sandwich.

Anyway, as I said, from the time I was five my dad would take me across the street to McCarren Park and play catch with me and make me take batting practice for two hours at a time. My friends would come, and my dad would pay them 10 cents apiece to shag balls in the outfield while I hit. I remember a drill that I use today at my camps in which he would throw me plastic golf balls with holes in them that were not only smaller than a regular baseball, but they moved in all directions. It's a drill that makes you concentrate and forces you to keep your eye on the ball. Then he would throw me a regular-size Whiffle ball. It's the same size as a baseball, of course, but looks huge after the little golf balls, and I would crush it. This drill sounds very simplistic, but I can tell you it works.

My First Team

Though we lived in Brooklyn, then the home of the Dodgers, my favorite team was the Yankees, so my first uniform number was 5, just like Joe DiMaggio, my father's favorite player. When I got older, I played for Our Lady of Mount Carmel's team in the Catholic Youth Organization, where I had a coach I will never forget. Nick Marino was an ex-marine, and he was built like the famous TV fitness guru Jack LaLanne. He was a short guy with muscles, short black hair, and a square chin. Nick's energy was unbelievable. To this day, when I have reached his age and consider myself in good shape, I can't believe that he coached almost all the teams we had at Our Lady, both in baseball and basketball.

The one big lesson he taught me—which I always stress to my players and students—is to give 100 percent at all times. Nick made us hustle in every drill that we did. It's no coincidence that we won championships almost every year. With the hustle that showed the other guys you cared, Nick taught us that your teammates can be your friends for life. When you're still a kid, you think you'll always see those guys you've grown up with and played ball with. But friendships grow stronger through shared hardship, or I should say shared struggle. When you play together as a team, you have to give up a little bit of yourself for the other guy. You don't realize it at the time, but when you see each other years later, and you've met so many people who pass by without affecting you, then you really cherish those shared moments. Seeing those guys that you haven't visited with for a while, the first thing you talk about is your playing days together.

For instance, years later when I'd get together with guys I played baseball with at St. Francis Prep, we'd always talk about when we had to walk to McCarren Park for practice, and we would have to walk past the public high school, Eli Whitney, right down the block. The old story in those days, you know, was that the kids from public school were dumber than the kids from Catholic school, dumb as that sounds. I doubt any of us really believed it, but it made for some solidarity. They had a lot of tough kids, and they used to make fun of us. So we would always fight them. Every week, there would be a fight. So that's what we always talk about.

On the streets where we ran around then, there were drugs. Some kids I knew, that I played ball with, I knew they were doing stuff. You could see when they were out of it. I told myself that I didn't want to ever get like that. I guess athletics kept me away from some of the bad stuff around me. Some of those guys I knew then are dead now, and some others aren't much better off.

At times, Nick pushed me more than my father did. And while I sometimes had to stop and gasp for air, I saw the improvement. I'm not saying I didn't listen to my father. He started me on the right path. He retired from his job early so he could watch me play ball my last two years in college. When he died I was in spring training with the Yankees, in 1982, so he got to see my World Series ring.

But Nick was a real coach. Sometimes you need that other person. A lot of kids come to my camps now, and their fathers say to me, "I'm sending him to you because he listens to you more than he listens to me." Nick was a real coach, and he was involved with us around a lot of other players. So we had to do it as a team, rather than as an individual. A father is interested in just his child, mostly. He loves his kid, and he goes to games to watch his kid. A coach has to mold a team, and there's a difference. As a player, you're more a cog in the machine, and you have to be to be a better ballplayer. It helped that Nick knew what he was talking about.

Number One at Eight

While I was in grammar school, I must have had newspaper articles written about my accomplishments daily. I'll never forget when I was in the Greenpoint youth league and the *Greenpoint Star* reported that I was the number one pick in the draft of the players after try-outs. I think I was eight years old. I first made the newspapers in 1962. It was a proud day in the Scala household.

It wasn't just that I could play that made me a number one pick. During the tryouts, we were playing a simulated game and I was playing third base. There was a man at third, and the batter hit a swinging bunt that I grabbed. I glanced at the guy on third, turned and faked the throw to first, and the man on third broke for the plate. He ran right into my tag. He was right there. They said, "Not only can this kid play the game, but he's got game smarts—at his age." I can remember that play still. I fielded the ball and the coach at third yelled, "stay, stay, stay," and then, when I faked the throw, he yelled, "go, go, go." I actually faked the coach out, too.

I played in three summer leagues every year in those days, taking myself to games sometimes. I would go from an afternoon game to a late afternoon game to a night game. I played with kids two and three years older than I was and was still the best player on the team. Some parents ask me if I believe in their kids playing up, above their age group, and I tell them as long as they can handle it, why not?

After playing baseball, football, and basketball at St. Francis Preparatory School in Brooklyn, I went to St. John's University on a full baseball scholarship and played four years.

My path to St. John's wasn't a very direct path, although it could have been. I took a little detour. At St. John's, I met two people who became instrumental in my life. The first was my wife, Yolanda. The other I'm getting to.

I was in my sophomore year at St. Francis when Jack Kaiser first indicated he wanted me to play for his prestigious baseball program at St. John's University, one of the premier schools in the East. The thing was, I was also playing high school football, and I was a pretty good all-around athlete. I was offered scholarships to some big-time schools, like Notre Dame, the University of Maryland, North Carolina State, Ohio State, and many others. I was overwhelmed, but I eventually chose to play football at Maryland and signed a letter of intent early in 1972.

I had yet to play baseball that spring as a senior at St. Francis Prep, and I had a tremendous season, breaking Joe Torre's offensive records, including the highest batting average in New York City Catholic High School history (.682). (You no doubt know Joe as the longtime manager of champion New York Yankee teams, but he was also an All-Star catcher, third baseman, and first baseman, a Most Valuable Player in the National League, and one of the best clutch hitters in major league baseball.) With that kind of season, I had to start thinking again. Should I play football or baseball?

I even got a call from the Atlanta Braves. They said they were thinking about drafting me, even though I had said I was going to play college football. The situation got muddier. Remember, I was only a high school senior, with my whole life ahead of me. My father told the Braves that they would have to do better than my college scholarship—and then some. The Braves passed, and I wasn't drafted out of high school.

So I headed off to College Park, Maryland, that August after senior year for my first college football practice. After a week, I knew I'd made the wrong decision back in the cold of January. I quit and headed back to Brooklyn. I decided that baseball was my true love. I came home, and that's when Jack Kaiser reentered my life.

I was home for a few days, and my father and my uncle knew a guy named Jimmy MacElroy, who was the baseball coach at St. Francis College. (Jimmy still sends me players. He's no longer at St. Francis, but he's still a figure in Brooklyn baseball.) He knew I was home and said to my father, "Why don't you bring him over" to an end-of-the-season all-star baseball game at Victory Field in Queens. Jimmy was there, and so was Jack Kaiser, scouting players for their college programs.

Jack came over and said hello, and then later said to me, "Why don't you come to my office, tomorrow?"

I said, "Yeah, sure, why not."

So I went to his office. I guess he checked my eligibility and made sure I had an NCAA release from Maryland and was eligible to play in the regular season. He could have said to me, "You know what, Dom, how about you come to St. John's, you pay for college this year, and we'll see how you do." But he respected the way I played the game. And, it could be, he felt that other colleges had begun to pick up that I was back—for instance, Jimmy MacElroy at St. Francis might be sniffing around. Jack Kaiser had been sending me letters since my sophomore year, to go play ball there, and I always liked St. John's. It was an offer I couldn't turn down.

Coach Kaiser became my mentor. He is the man who represented St. John's in baseball like Lou Carnesseca did in basketball. Both men are legends. To this day, they are both good friends of mine, and I speak to them often.

Coach Kaiser taught me that every situation is different in its own way. Anything can happen at any time. Every at bat is very important. Every pitch a pitcher throws is important. Each moment counts. A player may not get any hits in the game, but may make an important play in the field that will save two runs. So as a player, you never know what you're going to do to help the team win.

Now that I am a college baseball coach I've learned to be more patient—pretty patient, anyway. I can understand physical mistakes, but when a player keeps making mental mistakes, especially after the coach has been over them many times, that's the only time I get impatient. Physical mistakes you can't do much about. If you play the game, you know it's not easy, and nobody's trying to make a physical mistake. But mental mistakes are nothing but concentration, as far as missing signs or not understanding a play, and that means the player is not thinking about the play beforehand. Players must stay focused and try not to be detrimental to their team. They must think where they need to be given any possible outcome of the next pitch, and then they can be there.

Coach Kaiser was always positive and tried to help his players in all our many situations and youthful dilemmas. He believed that all of a team's players should be an asset to the team. I was very fortunate to be around him. I'm a better coach and person because of him.

In college, I was elected captain my senior year and led the team in all offensive categories. I was 15th in the nation in batting average (.420) and was selected as a third-team All-American. I also received the Peter Smith Award as St. John's Most Valuable Player. Unfortunately, we were beaten in the regionals of the NCAA Tournament by Seton Hall University, who then advanced to the College World Series. (That team was led by Rick Cerone, a catcher who became my teammate and good friend a few years down the road when he took the place of one of my good friends and teammates with the Yankees—captain Thurman Munson, the All-Star catcher who died in a plane crash far too early in life.)

All the years of hard work and dedication, of playing in the hot summer weather when many of my friends were at the beach or going to barbecues, finally paid off.

I'll never forget the date: it's like my birthday almost. On June 5, 1976, I was at St. John's, taking batting practice with some team-mates, getting my licks in. My father called the school and asked for me. Someone came out to get me, and my father said that I had a phone call from Ralph DiLullo, the area scout for the Oakland A's. I'd been drafted by the A's in the sixth round of the amateur draft, the 125th player selected. I was numb. I knew I had a chance to make it as a professional ballplayer.

I jumped in my car, and I don't remember driving home. I was on a cloud. The only thing I remember is speaking to Charlie Finley, the legendary owner of the A's. I signed for $15,000, plus incentives. How's that for a dream come true?

Lee Mazzilli

I've known Lee since our high school days, and we are still good friends today. Lee played at Lincoln High School, so we didn't play them in the spring, but all the great players played in the infamous Parade Ground League. Many greats, such as Joe Torre, Joe Pepitone, Rico Petrocelli, John Candelaria, and Willie Randolph graced the spacious diamonds there. This was the Cape Cod League of Brooklyn for high school players.

There are some great stories out of this league, and I have one that involves Lee Mazzilli. Lee was a slender speedster who had all the tools to be a future big-league player. He was not only a switch-hitter, but he was ambidextrous. He played first base lefty and center field righty. When I saw this, I said, "Wow, he is unreal."

He was a great line-drive hitter and, for his size, hit the ball as hard as anyone in the league. And he could fly around the bases with ease. You can attribute that to his championship-caliber speed skating on the ice. He had great legs, and that's why he hit the ball so hard. It is what we teach in this book: use your back side (legs) to get your power to hit.

On a very steamy Sunday, we played Lee's team on the famous Diamond 7 in the Parade Grounds. There were more than 20 scouts in the stands that day, and I was on the opposite end, playing third base. It is funny, but I remember that the scouts were no big deal; we'd just go out and play the game that we loved so much.

Lee had a great game, hitting, running, and sliding so gracefully. But that day I happened to open some scouts' eyes also. In the doubleheader (two seven-inning games), I laced two home runs and two doubles and had eight runs batted in.

After that game, 10 scouts came up to me and had me fill out cards for the upcoming draft. I was on the map. The Atlanta Braves wanted to draft me, but I had already committed to the

University of Maryland to play college football. They decided not to waste a pick because I wasn't going to sign.

Still, it was a great feeling and a preview of what was going to happen four years later. Lee, thank you for bringing them out.

It is funny, but to this day, I tell my players that story. When Bobby Lanigan (third-round pick in the 2008 draft from Adelphi) was being scouted, I told the players that you never know who is watching; they may see something else that they like.

Years later, I had a hard time distracting Lee Mazzilli from intently watching his own son play ball. There's nothing like a father at his son's ball game, suffering the thrill of victory and the agony of defeat right along with him. Baseball for many of us is a father-and-son game; many of us come to baseball from our fathers' passion for the game. Former Chicago White Sox manager Gene Lamont (whom you'll hear from later in this book) has a son playing professional ball. He learned from his dad, and I learned from mine. It's certainly not the only way to get started, but for some families it's a tradition that binds generations.

Lee was a longtime Mets and New York fan favorite. He played 14 seasons in the big leagues, hitting .303 with 15 home runs and 76 RBI in 1979 for the Mets. He was traded to the Yankees in August 1982, when I was coaching there, and stayed just until after the season when the Yanks traded him to Pittsburgh. He came back to the Mets in 1986 and helped them win the World Series. After retiring from playing, Lee stepped into coaching for the Yankees, and then he managed the Baltimore Orioles for a couple of years before coming back to the Yankees as Joe Torre's bench coach in 2006. He is currently a studio analyst for Sports-Net New York, the Mets' network.

Here are some of Lee's tips for young players and their coaches on hitting and playing the game.

Have Fun

My first piece of advice for young players is make sure you're having a lot fun playing baseball. It's important to love what you're doing. When you're young, the most important thing is to get out there and play. Don't think about making mistakes. Don't be afraid to fail. You have to fail before you can succeed. That's what I tell young kids. If you strike out, that's okay. It's not the worst thing in the world.

As you get older, you'll get more refined with your abilities. It'll get easier. You'll be surprised at the changes. You go from hitting off your dad throwing underhanded, to hitting off the tee, to batting practice—things of that nature.

Sacrifice Beyond the Fly Ball

One of the biggest things I learned coming up as a ballplayer? Sacrifice. There's a lot of sacrificing in baseball. We're not talking about the bunt sacrifice. We're talking about sacrificing for the game. Playing high school ball, going on to college, if you want to be successful, this is something where you really have to put in the work. If you can't sacrifice, you're gone. . . . I remember when I was a kid and my friends were going to the beach or a barbecue on Saturday and Sunday, I was out there in Marine Park or the Parade Grounds, sweating my buns off playing five games a weekend. That's sacrifice.

Hitting

Be aware that when you get to sandlot baseball, or high school baseball, the kids can get overwhelmed by hitting. They all want to hit home runs. One of the things they need to work on is making consistent, hard contact and hitting the ball with authority. Tell the kids that if they're doing that, the home runs will come. Tell them, "Don't try to hit home runs. Hit the ball with authority." That's the most important thing.

How do you ensure hard contact? A lot of batting practice, and hitting off the tee. In practice, try to hit consistent, hard line drives up the middle, use the gaps, hit the ball gap to gap. The home runs will come.

Pitch selection is key. Be patient at the plate, and be aggressive when you get a pitch to hit. And don't be afraid to hit with two strikes.

Patience

If you are working with and developing young players, the most important thing to have is patience. A coach needs to know that, at times, young kids are unaware of the proper way to do things; it's not so much that they don't have the skill, they just don't know. You have to be ready to teach all the time. You have to teach the game every day. Have patience with young kids.

2

Getting Started: Perfect Practice Makes Perfect

L ike all the games we love from the playground or empty lot, baseball is a team sport. Although, at its heart, the game comes down to a pitcher battling a batter, most people don't think of it as a one-on-one sport. The way I coach and teach the game, baseball is very much a one-on-one sport, especially for young players. That's why I always try to have almost as many instructors working with kids as I have kids, so that each player is shown the fundamentals of the game as much as possible, over and over again, until he gets it right.

Whether the player is batting, pitching, or fielding, he needs to learn the importance of good technique by repeating drills, then repeating them again. Only then can he truly learn the game. I always say, "Perfect practice makes perfect." This is what I preach at my camps for young or beginning players and high school players, and at the college where I coach.

Organizers of youth baseball have a tough job. They've got to find enough adults with enough time away from their normal, demanding jobs to spend time with kids and teach them to play baseball. And it takes a lot of time and commitment. It's true some folks are coaches who aren't qualified to coach, and they may be there because they want their own children to get the benefit of the doubt with regard to playing time. Maybe they have less than perfect motives, but at the same time, you have to give them credit for giving the time to their kids.

We have to remember that the baseball field belongs primarily to the players. I have always felt that coaches should be watched to see what kind of instructions they are giving the kids under their supervision. There are several basic rules, but first and foremost is that the players should have fun. We can't forget that it's just a game.

Rich "Goose" Gossage, the great relief pitcher for the New York Yankees and 2008 Hall of Fame inductee, says that some of his greatest baseball memories come from the time he played in Little League. "My coaches always kept it simple," he says. "They would stress the fundamentals until we got them down."

That's a powerful word—fundamentals. It means the basics. It's a very important step in learning the game. We tell our children, "Hey, go to school and learn the fundamentals—or the basics—in all your classes. If you don't learn the basics, you can't go to the next level." This is as true of baseball as it is in every other pursuit.

Getting a Feel for It

Here are some basic fundamentals I stress at One-on-One Baseball camp.

I find it incredible that many kids don't know how to properly hold a baseball and throw it. What my instructors and I teach our students is not only how to do certain basic things, but why to do them. I feel it's critical that young players understand why they're asked to do things and then develop the feel for doing them the right way.

For example, in throwing the baseball: Why do you make sure you pick up and grip a ground ball with four seams, instead of just grabbing it and throwing it across the infield? Why should you take a "crow hop"—a quick move with both feet—and follow through after you throw the ball?

When a coach teaches any part of the game, there should be a reason for teaching the lesson. Once you explain and demonstrate a point, the player does it. I always ask my players, "Do you see and feel what I'm talking about?" This is the case at every level of baseball, youth league, high school, summer ball, college, and professional. We all need to understand why we do things a certain way.

Let's go back now and understand the basics of fielding a ground ball and throwing it. The reason for gripping the ball with four seams is that the throw will have more spin and carry with authority to the guy getting the throw. If you grip the ball with two seams, it will sink and move, and that will almost always result in an errant throw. And if you throw the ball flat-footed instead of taking that crow hop, the ball will dive and have no power behind it.

Why do we call this move a crow hop? If you watch a crow walk, you will see that he hops along with short strides. After you field a grounder or catch a fly ball, your first step should be a crow hop. It gives you momentum to throw the ball with power.

These steps are simple and basic, yet there are kids who don't understand them until you make them feel them and do them. I see kids come to camp who don't know how to approach a ground ball or how to go back on a fly ball. They watch the Yankees' Derek Jeter come in and scoop up grounders like an acrobat on the run, and they try to emulate him. They don't see what he does in practice before the game, where he—and the other major leaguers they watch on television—take hundreds of ground balls the basic way, the routine right way. I call this the "TV effect." The young players don't understand the reality of this. They only do what they see.

Extraordinary plays come from players who have made the routine part of their muscle memory through practice.

A Prescription for Fundamentals

In the week before games, coaches don't have many hours for their teams to practice. That's why they should have an organized schedule. The following is how I organize practice time for my college team at Adelphi University.

It depends on whether we have to practice inside when it's cool out, or outside, but a lot of times we'll work on something we didn't do well in the last game. Let's say we messed up a bunt play in a game. The next practice we'll go over that so we cut down on our mistakes the next time. If we're not hitting in situations, we'll go over and do some situational batting practice. We'll put the guys in certain counts and we'll throw certain pitches, and they'll try to jump on the pitch.

Each week you should go over fundamentals. It's not all about batting practice. Teach something new—like relays between outfielders and infielders. This is a basic aspect of play, but often is critical in helping a team win a game.

Create simulated situations with runners on base so that your infielders and outfielders know where to throw the ball in any given play. You'll be amazed at how this simple drill will help come game time.

Work on baserunning—how to cut the bases, make simple turns between bases. Teach the players to look at the coaches if they're thinking of trying to take an extra base. I am always perplexed by the number of young players who don't have this basic training. If players are taught these lessons at a young age, these lessons will stay with them forever.

If a high school coach is picking between two players to make a team and one has more raw talent but the other one has good, sound fundamentals, the coach will invariably choose the player who knows the basics. That player will most likely have a better understanding of what it takes to become a better player.

In later chapters, I'll go into more detail with drills I consider basic, as well as critical, for players trying to advance their knowledge and understanding of the game and reach the next level. But first, there must be a commitment to learning and understanding. It's encouraging that in the past five years, more and more youngsters are playing baseball. Thanks to major league stars like Derek Jeter and David Wright who have dedicated themselves to the game they love and enjoy, young players are getting back to emulating their heroes.

Setting the Tone

Commitment is a strong word. It goes with dedication and perspiration. Willie Randolph was an All-Star second baseman with the New York Yankees and the Los Angeles Dodgers and went on to become manager of the New York Mets. He thinks the commitment begins when a player is 7 to 10 years old. That's when a kid finds out if he truly loves the game.

"I remember as a boy getting up for eight o'clock games on Saturday mornings," Willie says. "There were times when it was 40 degrees out and windy, but you went to the park and played. No one had to push me to get out of bed and go."

Commitment is the most important part not only of baseball, but of life itself, in what determines success for what you want to accomplish. You have to be totally committed to what you do in order to succeed. I had some of the guys over to my house to dinner the other night, my captains and seniors, and I told them, "Do you know, when I was younger, when I went to high school and college, I really didn't know what a barbecue was. Literally, I knew what it was, but I really didn't know what it was like to go to a barbecue and spend the whole day, sit down and have a hamburger, have a hot dog, then stop, and later have a steak and a sausage and peppers, stuff like that. I never had the time, because I was always playing ball. I was committed to excelling, and I wanted to be a major league baseball player."

That may seem crazy to some, but it's what it takes. You can't get there with halfway measures. You can't improve unless you give it your all, and believe me, it may take a little more out of you than you think you want, but there's a certain high that makes it worth it. I'm not talking about the major leagues, I'm talking about excellence. There's a tingle in your head that isn't there with mediocrity, and that high is a lot more useful than any drug I know of.

The Five Stations

Whether kids are pitching, throwing, or hitting, they have to be able to feel the effect of good technique. Practice—repetition the right way—builds muscle memory. Just as we reflexively walk without thinking about it, the great athletes hit a baseball 400 feet without thinking about it. So it's best to keep them at it.

Each practice should include work on what I call baseball's five stations:

- Pitching
- Hitting (beginning players should start from a tee)
- Fielding ground balls and pop-ups in the infield
- Catching fly balls and ground balls in the outfield
- Running the bases

Divide the kids up and keep them working at one of the five spots on the practice field. It'll keep their attention, and you won't have minds wandering off. You'll improve their focus and their enthusiasm because they're always getting to do something instead of standing around. Practice may get to be more fun for them than games if you keep it lively.

Before a camp or practice session can begin, there needs to be preparation. Is the field ready for the players? Is enough time being budgeted to learn and practice what must be accomplished? Is all the proper equipment available? Do the players show up ready to absorb what they need to absorb? Are the coaches and instructors ready to impart their knowledge of the game efficiently and patiently?

A regular and consistent practice schedule should be maintained. This is necessary to sustain interest and enthusiasm for everyone, player and instructor.

Athleticism

Every player has a different level of athletic ability. Not everyone is Alex Rodriguez or Johan Santana. Some kids are just natural athletes, they're born with it. But nearly every player can benefit from drills in agility, coordination, and strength, including fielding and baserunning.

These include the following:

- Sprints
- Leg crossovers
- Drills that develop hand-eye coordination
- Agility drills
- Leg strengthening
- Fielding the ball quickly
- Quick bursts

Baseball is a game of quickness much more than brawn. You've probably heard the baseball announcer's clichéd comment so many times that's it's almost a nursery rhyme: "Baseball is a game of inches." It is, isn't it? How many plays have you seen where the batter is just out at first base? Barely a blink of an eye. And umpires rarely get it wrong in the majors. Whoever came up with the 90-foot dimensions sure hit a magic number.

Don't think that when summer is over it's time to put away your baseball. There may be a regular schedule of games at one time of the year, but baseball isn't a seasonal sport. Preparation and practice goes on year-round once players reach the college level, but why wait that long? Weight training was once considered ill conceived for baseball players, but modern trainers have learned enough about physiology to develop specific programs for ballplayers. The young guys shouldn't be lifting weights too early, but everybody needs to stay in shape with plenty of exercise in the off-season.

Tell your hitters to keep swinging that bat through the fall and winter. They should go down to the basement, find a spot where they won't hit any of their mom's lamps or other precious things, and swing 100 times a day. That way they won't lose that muscle memory come spring.

Pitchers can practice their motion with a dish towel in their pitching hand, throwing it as if it were the ball (it should snap to the floor). Instruct them to do this 10 times with each pitch they throw in four or five sets, resting a few minutes between sets. They'll have a more consistent motion in the spring, and it won't take nearly as long to shake the rust off.

Each of these exercises will take your players no more than 10 minutes a day, in addition to a short regular course of exercise. They greatly improve muscle memory and preserve what you taught your players last summer.

Coda

There's a famous, funny scene in the movie *Bull Durham.* Well, there are a lot of famous, funny scenes in that movie, mostly because it's full of baseball clichés. But there is no greater baseball commandment than that delivered by the exasperated manager to his misfit Durham Bulls: "It's a simple game: you throw the ball; you catch the ball; you hit ball."

The devil may be in the details, but in the long run, and in the games that count, it's the team that executes the fundamentals of the game that wins. The team that practices infield and outfield, the team that always throws to the right base, the team that doesn't throw the ball away, the team that gets the bunt down, that moves the runner over, that turns every double play, that doesn't give up on an at bat, that doesn't give in to a hitter who's fouled off the last nine two-strike pitches, that doesn't give in to the pitcher who's thrown nine tough two-strike pitches, the team that fights to the last out when they're losing by six runs. That team wins, because that team probably sticks together, because that team knows how to win. It's certain that team is properly schooled in fundamentals, and they practice them until dark.

Perhaps, too, they may sometimes slide together in man-made mud puddles, but don't tell their mothers.

The Day I Got Hurt

I was in the A's organization and we were in Chattanooga, Tennessee, playing against the Atlanta Braves affiliate at the time. It was about the eighth inning. It was an 8–8 game. I was catching. It was a hot night. The sweat—I can remember it to this day. You sweat profusely out there, catching eight innings, in the heat, in Tennessee, in July or August. I was nice and loose and playing well. I believe I was one for three, and I had gotten a nice hit before that and scored a run. We had a runner on third and one out. There were about 8,000 people in the stands. Of course, they were all cheering, and it was a big game. I got up and hit a 2-2 pitch, a long fly ball to center field, and it was caught at the warning track. The guy came in and scored from third, and all my teammates were slapping me five when I came back from running to first.

Then we were winning 9–8 and going into the bottom of the ninth. And being a guy who wears the game on his sleeve, I was psyched up, I was ready to go. And of course, the scenario now was, to make a long story short, they got a man on, they bunted him over. I don't know how the guy got to third, but it was one out with a man on third. And the same thing happened. A guy got up and hit a fly ball to center field. The guy was tagging.

Now, I was taught to block home plate, but—and I teach this today to my catchers and to my kids—you have to show him a little bit of the plate, because you don't want to get run over. That's not what you're trying to do in baseball. So what you do is you have your feet on the corners of the base, your heels on the corners of home plate, waiting for the throw. Being in your athletic position, seeing which way you're going to go.

The ball happened to be coming a little bit up the right side, so I saw the throw was going to be off a little bit. I knew we weren't going to get him, but I was still in this position. I kind of came up away, because I was going to cut the throw. I was going to give him the plate. I was not going to block the plate, not going to get hurt for no reason. But as he was crossing the plate standing up, because he knew there wasn't going to be a play, he tried to come across and hit me with an elbow. He nicked a corner of my eye. He would have really got me solid if I hadn't moved. And being hot tempered, and Italian, I went after him after he crossed home plate. I grabbed him by the back of his shirt and threw him over me. Actually, he was looking at me at the time. He was just turning around to go back to the third-base dugout, and I grabbed him and we started fighting and tussling. I threw him down. Of course, a big fight broke out. They threw me out of the game. They threw him out, too. I felt a little twinge in my shoulder, but I thought nothing of it. We actually won the game. I got thrown out, but we won the game.

I must have lost 8 to 10 pounds sweating that night catching, so I hit the showers, went out with the guys, and all in all felt pretty good. The next day, I got up and felt a little twinge, but I still didn't think anything of it.

I went to the ballpark, and I went to throw the ball, and I couldn't throw it 10 feet. I tried to play catch with a guy about 20 feet away, just getting loose. I tried to throw the ball, and it wouldn't go. That's when I found out what I had. It was called torn ligaments in those days, but now it's called a torn rotator cuff.

The tough thing was that I had a great arm. That was one of my best assets as a catcher. The A's moved me from third base to catcher because they needed a catcher. And I said that I would catch. I loved the position. I was a natural behind the plate. I needed work blocking balls, but not a lot got by me, because I had good hands. The first guy I ever threw out was in a scrimmage game in spring training in the minor leagues: Rickey Henderson, when we were both coming up with the A's. There was a left-handed pitcher on the mound, so he held him a little closer, but I threw a seed down there, right on the money. He was out by like two feet, wasn't even close.

I was hurt, out the rest of that year, and then came back the next February to spring training. Charlie Finley was selling the A's at that time. He tried to sell Vida Blue, but the commissioner wouldn't let him sell Vida Blue. So they made a nine-for-two-player trade. They sent Vida Blue to the Giants, and the Giants sent nine players, and two of those players were catchers. I was still caught in the Double-A and Triple-A in-between syndrome. They moved guys and figured out what they had, and they released me. That's when the Yankees picked me up for their bull pen, and I started my career with the Yankees.

3
How We Run Our Camps

Every summer, I gather my college staff to help as instructors in a baseball camp I run in Garden City, New York, across from Adelphi. We also have camps in the heart of Queens, a real pretty place if you haven't been there before. (A lot of television shows and tourist excursions never get off the island of Manhattan when they're in New York City, which is a shame.) I bring in a lot of kids—more than 500—every year, from the little guys six years old to high school–age kids, and many of our student-athletes come back year after year. We have a good time, we get hot and sweaty, we play games all day, and at the end of the week, we've all learned something about baseball and teamwork.

To give you an idea of our approach to One-on-One Baseball, I'll give you a walk-through of a typical day and the week in camp. If you're a coach working with kids of different ages, or different talent levels, you can use our program as a template to design your own practice schedule.

Day 1 Begins

We start out the first-day gathering about 8:15 in the morning and begin the program at 9:00. Before 9:00, the kids check in, and everybody gets a name tag and a T-shirt. The kids are told to wear the shirts on the second day and the last day of camp so that everybody looks like and feels like a group. With the kids gathered together on the bleachers at our fields, I let them know all our rules and regulations and what we're trying to accomplish, the goals we're trying to meet while they're there, how we're going to make them better players, and we introduce the staff.

At 9:30, we start our calisthenics. Picture about 60 or 70 kids on the field, including the rookies (usually ages 7 to 9), the minors (ages 10 to 12), and our majors (ages 13 to 15). After some simple calisthenics, we start our running; we do regular sprints, then we go into karaoke (foot-over-foot) and agility drills. After that, we do high-leg drills to get blood flowing, the legs good and loose. We do about five different methods of sprinting. We'll also do backpedal/side-pedal drills, on the whistle, to improve players' agility.

Then we get the bases out and form six lines. We tell the kids, "If you never knew how to slide, you're going to learn how to slide before you end this camp." We slide every day. With the little kids on the first day, we just want them to get the idea of running the proper way and how to dig in and slide. The main operating principle is to run hard. By the fourth day, on Thursday, we have a sliding contest. We eliminate people until we have our sliding champion, who will be recognized at the end of camp.

After we do our running, the first day is an evaluation day. We don't play any games the first day. It's all drills and batting practice

High-leg drills

and stuff like that, the things you'd normally find at tryouts for your local youth league. The instructors get an idea of who we have and how we can divide up the kids to make the teams fair for the camp's afternoon sessions, when we play games. The kids will stay on the same teams every day, and then on the last day, we play championship games in each age division, with round robins taking into account the records from the rest of the week.

Generally the groups are divided into the divisions I mentioned previously. We do take some six-year-olds if we think they can handle it. It's a long day, a lot of baseball. It takes a lot of stamina for a little guy, so aside from his ability at that age, you want to know if he can take the whole day. You don't want him to think it's work.

Basic Drills

After everybody does stretching and running, the rookies go to our back field, where they will work on more fundamental things. The younger kids have to be taught separately, more fundamental skills. Even though everything we preach is fundamentals, the older kids are ready for a little bit more advanced skills training than the younger guys. You can't have young, young kids feeling lost. So we separate kids for the most part, and I'll go back and forth between the groups.

PROPER THROWING. Now that we're separated, we'll loosen up, emphasizing proper throwing, holding the ball across the seams, using the legs, bringing the arm back and following the throw through. Our guys watch to see how the kids throw: whether they baby the ball, whether they start from the wrong foot, that sort of thing. We show them the proper way right off the get-go, to draw their arm back and cock the ball behind the ear, step toward the target, and snap off a four-seam throw, letting the arm follow through across the body.

QUICK HANDS. This drill is probably the most help for the minors, the kids in the preteen years, but it's good for everybody. It's like a quick around-the-horn you would do on the infield after an out. The guys stand about 10 to 15 feet apart. Each player gets the ball, and as he's receiving it—with two hands—he turns and throws it to the next guy. It's similar to a shortstop or second baseman turning a double play. An infielder should be able to do that. Third baseman, same way. He gets the ball, he throws it, boom. Every drill that we do has a purpose.

FOUR-MAN RELAY DRILL. Another important drill that we repeat throughout the week is the relay throw. Four guys get in a long line, the number of feet of separation depends on the age group. This is a drill everybody has to do, because when you are playing in a game, whether you're an outfielder or an infielder, you always have to take a throw on your glove side and throw to the other. If the throw is a little off-line, do you get the ball and turn the opposite way? No, because that takes too much time and you have to throw across your body. You use quick feet, adjust, then turn and throw to the next guy. So there are two things the players are learning. They're learning to give the proper throw to the cutoff man, and they're also learning how to get the cutoff throw. If you watch the pros, you won't see them turning clockwise to throw to another base. That's another three seconds. That's the difference between "out" and "safe," sometimes. Every throw, every step we take in practice, has a purpose for the game.

Sometimes we'll stop the guys in the middle of a game and say, "See what we're talking about? On the relay throw, you made a nice throw. You make your throw off-side, boom." We do a lot of that stuff.

The Five Stations

At one point then, we gather everybody, minors and majors, in the center.

I get out the posters: I believe pictures are worth a thousand words. I have assembled action photographs of big-league players and college guys—all of them of them doing one particular baseball skill the right way.

We separate the kids into five groups:

- We have a group for baserunning. The baserunning station teaches the players to run past the bag on infield grounders and how to make the proper turn if the ball is hit to the outfield.
- There's a group for hitting off of the tees. I have three or four tees, and we have a number of drills that instill the proper mechanics of a good swing.
- We have an infield instructor, hitting ground balls to short-stop and second base. The emphasis here is on getting in the proper position to field a ball, hands out in front, with the alligator technique (one hand is positioned over the other, and they snap shut on the ball like an alligator's jaws). They'll see a picture of Alex Rodriguez going after the ball, two hands, one hand on top of the other. Here's a shortstop going for the ball, one hand on top of the other. Sure, they're superstars, but they make routine plays the proper way, every day, dozens of ground balls a day.
- We'll have a pitching station.
- And we'll have an outfield station, where a machine helps show the players the proper way to get under a fly ball.

Everybody gets 15 minutes on each station. If we have 60 campers, that's a dozen kids at each station. The whistle blows and they rotate. They know what our objectives are at each position.

While the minors and majors are doing that, the rookies are doing a little more fundamental stuff: catching and throwing, proper grips, hitting off tees.

Hitting and the "Wrinkle Effect"

With the hitters, I'll show the guys pictures of big leaguers. "Guys have different stances," I say, "but when the ball is coming to the plate, everybody has to be in the proper loading position. You can start here like Gary Sheffield does, but you have to load here, like everybody who can hit does. The next thing you have to have is good arm extension, all the way through the baseball. That's something that all of these guys do."

And I ask them, "What's one thing that all of these guys have? Do you see that? Big Papi, here?" Usually somebody knows, but I emphasize for them all: "Heads down on the ball, chin to the shoulder."

That's a thing we work on with tees. We'll work especially on that on the tees. It's obvious to say, but it's easily the most common mistake.

"Remember, if you can't see it, you can't hit it," I say. "You have to have good balance, proper extension, head down, and a good follow-through."

The follow-through is just as important as the rest, and there is a good way to look to see if a player is doing it right. I call it the wrinkle effect. I point it out in the photographs I have mounted on my poster board. As you look at the pants of a guy who is hitting the ball properly with the right power, there are wrinkles on the right side—or the left side for left-handed hitters—of the player's pants. That's when you can tell a guy is hitting the ball well, balanced, following through and hitting with authority.

That takes up the morning.

Day 1 Afternoon

The minor-league guys go to one field, and major-league guys go to another. We keep the kids busy so their attention doesn't waver. We don't want anybody standing around with nothing to do or feeling left out. Our instructors keep an eye out for little glitches in a kid's game, and we'll take them aside and show them the proper way. Everybody has something, some area where they didn't quite get it right the first time, but the sooner those things are corrected and followed by practice and repetition, the better they should become, with good technique as ingrained as bicycle riding.

After a break for lunch, we hit the field again that first day, and we continue to evaluate the players. Each guy gets about 15 swings. At the same time, we're still evaluating the pitching, because we want to make sure the teams are equal, which makes for better games. You don't want one team with all the sharpest pitchers. Pitching coaches watch the players, make sure they throw strikes, and instruct them in proper mechanics. The next morning, the instructors will hold a draft. We're also aware of personalities and try to put together guys who will play better as a team with each other.

Base Hits and Defense

If we have time that first day, we play a game of base hits and defense. We have an offensive team and a defensive team. The offensive team gets a point when they hit the ball hard, or when they get a hit. If they hit it over a defensive guy's head, they get another point. In the field, if a guy makes a great play, he gets points on defense. If he makes a routine play, he gets one point, because you have got to make the routine plays. Great plays are all fine and good, and we applaud them, but routine plays *have* to be made. We emphasize that. Three outs is enough for one inning; you hate to give them four outs, which is what you're doing when you don't make that routine play.

Day 2 Morning

We start the second day very much like the first. We stretch, do our calisthenics, and slide. Every day begins with "stretch and slide, stretch and slide." We separate again. The rookies again go over more basic things. It's important that they go over and over the basics.

Pop-Up Drill

The minors now get a pop-up drill. How many times have you seen kids that age struggle with pop-ups? You'll see a young kid stand out to the side of a pop and wave his glove at it. We have a machine that uses a soft ball so they won't get hurt if they miss. They have to stay under the ball. It's called a Lite-Flight Machine, and it lobs the yellow soft ball into the air for them. First, we have them catch the ball with just their bare hands so they have to use two hands. They get used to reaching for the ball rather than sticking a glove out and hoping it falls into it. Then we have them catch it with the glove. This way, they get a good idea of what the proper approach to a pop-up is. They get under the ball.

Defensive Drills

We have other defensive drills. The minors and majors on their separate fields form four lines, one behind each of the infield positions. We ask, "What's your main position, and what's your second position," and we have them practice at both because they need to be able to move around the infield. We hit 15 minutes of straight ground balls at them. Then we'll make them go to their left, their right. We want to see their glove-side position, their crossover step. We have the shortstops and second basemen work on force plays. The shortstop gets the ball and flips it, the second baseman gets it and he flips it. While they're doing that, the third basemen are throwing over to first. We see if they can get their step, get the ball, get their crow hop, and get rid of it. We want to make sure they get their arms back.

Where to Go with the Ball

We do cutoffs and relays after the defensive drills, to make sure that when kids get in their games they know what to do with the baseball, because a lot of kids don't know. While we're doing that, the little kids are playing a game called "Where to Go with the Ball." A lot of these little guys at six, seven, or eight years old get the ball in the outfield, and what do you see them do? They hold it. They don't know what to do with it. So we go over it with them: "Nobody else on? Throw the ball to the second baseman or the shortstop and let him relay it to second base." We're telling them, many of them for the first time, how to do cutoffs and relays. It goes back and reinforces the relay drill that we do all the time.

We'll simulate situations. We want to teach players to start thinking about where they're going to throw the ball, given the current situation of the game, like "runners on first and third, one out," and so on, and recognize what their responsibilities are given anything that happens in the next play. Go over all the possibilities and make sure the players know where they are going to throw the ball should it come to them and where they should be to back up the play. It's all solid, sound baseball, but too often, nobody practices it enough.

Pitchers

Don't worry. Pitchers aren't left out. They throw every other day and go over fundamentals when they don't pitch. We pay attention to when they have to throw at night in their leagues. These kids get overworked as it is. We don't want to hurt them.

We keep everybody moving. When the majors are hitting in the cage, we'll have the minors doing fielding, and vice versa. We practice and demonstrate pickoff plays and teach them how to bunt. I think everybody should know how to bunt. We'll have catchers and middle infielders practicing throws to second, catchers working on signs and blocking balls in the dirt.

Day 2 Afternoon

At 1 P.M., we'll start our games. Rookies hit off coaches so they can run around, and when they're finished they'll learn how to run the bases.

We believe in a lot of batting practice, so the minors will hit off the machine in their games, but we'll have some pitching. It depends on how many people we have and who is available to pitch. Like I said, we're conscious of when they may have to pitch for their league teams. They'll play three-inning games, and the winner plays on, an extra game depending on how many people and teams we have.

Hitting off the machines makes things more uniform, gives the kids more strikes to hit, and moves the games along. We get a lot of good hitting in. With the majors, it's the same thing, or they will hit off the coaches. We're constantly stopping play to point out mistakes or praise good plays and lessons learned.

At 3 P.M., everybody runs the bases, and like every day, we do more sliding before it's time to head for the showers.

Days 3 and 4

Before we start our exercises and stretching on Wednesday, we'll talk about what we've learned so far, and sometimes we'll play a little game of baseball trivia. What fan doesn't enjoy putting one over on the other guys? Then, after stretching and sliding, we'll go into more of the same various drills.

We'll do outfield practice. We'll set the pitching machine up on the mound, and we'll hit fly balls with it. We usually put up a screen, and we make the outfielders hit a cutoff screen. They get points, and they play a game, one team against the other, how many guys can hit the screen with a nice line drive on a throw. These are good things, the way they play games, competitions. It keeps the kids going.

Another thing we'll do is set up the Lite-Flight Machine for hitting. (We have the pitching machine hitting and the fly ball machine pitching.) If the players don't keep their eyes on the ball with the Lite-Flight Machine, they'll never hit it. So they learn to stay down on the ball and not pull their head out. We also always have tees handy near screens on the side, and players are always hitting off the tees. All the time somebody seems to be hitting.

There are more situation practices and relays, defense on bunt plays, how to field with a bare hand. We put players on the bases in situations. We work on where to go with the ball: "If you're the third baseman and the ball is hit to your left, with runners on first and second, what do you do? A lot of guys try to turn around and beat the guy to third base for the force out, but you're heading the wrong way. So you should go to second for the double play." We try to go over all these little things that happen in the game. If the players have done them before, there's less to think about during a game.

Box Drills

Box drills improve hand-eye coordination. It's just tossing the ball from third base to second base to home to third base, and then in the opposite direction so players can get the ball and throw it from both sides. They learn the proper way to move, to move their feet, which is important.

Home Run Derby

Wednesday, we start our games in the afternoon. But on Thursday, we play the games a little earlier, and later we have a Home Run Derby, or so we call it, with the Lite-Flight Machine. We set it up so they can hit a home run. If they do, it's points for their team. It's another one of those games that kids just love to play, and they get something out of it: they keep their head down, they hit the ball the proper way. It's a real quick return. They get the points, and they get the team spirit.

Bunting

We'll also take a half hour and just practice bunting off the machine. It surprises me how many high school kids I see that don't know how to bunt. I've got kids coming to me in college who don't know how to bunt, which is terrible. Bunting is so much a part of the game—as this book is being written my team is just coming off of a win that happened on account of a bunt. In the bottom of the eighth inning of a 1–1 game, our leadoff guy bunted his way on base to start things off. We have a play in which the runner goes as soon as a left-handed pitcher lifts his leg. This pitcher was rattled and threw over the first baseman's head. Our leadoff guy went all the way to third. We got a sacrifice fly the next pitch. That made it 2–1, which held up as the final. So these are the little things that players have to learn.

We teach our players how to steal, the way to read the pitcher on a steal. We teach them how to tag up on a fly ball, where they should be looking, and how to catch a fly in the right position so that you can gun down a runner trying to advance. We teach the catcher the proper stance with a runner on base. There is a lot more to the game than batting practice and a little infield.

Day 5

Friday is usually a fun day. We play a lot of different games. After stretching and sliding, we set up two sets of agility tests. Older players run an obstacle course with cones, a ladder course, jumping up on a box, and hurdles.

Steal the Baseball

While the big kids are working on their agility, the younger kids play "Steal the Baseball." You line up two teams of eight guys apiece facing one another, and you put a baseball in the middle. It's just like "Steal the Bacon." You call out a number—three, for example—and whoever is number three on one side goes against number three on the other side. One guy has to grab the ball before the other guy tags it. It's about being athletic and quick. Baseball is about quick bursts.

Circle Drill

The circle drill has a coach in the middle, and there are about 10 guys in the circle and they have to go around sideways to their left. The coach keeps flipping the ball, and the players don't know where he's going to flip it, so they have to be quick. They have to have soft hands. They get a little dizzy, and it really can work out their legs.

Postgame

We'll finish up with some more defensive drills, and the rookies will have their Home Run Derby. Now, it's about 11 A.M., and it's been a long week for the rookies and they're usually a little tired. So I give them a break and have them watch the older kids play. I say, "Look at them. Pretty soon, that's going to be you out there."

After lunch, the parents come for the championship games, and we have our awards ceremony afterward. We talk about what everybody has done during the week and what they've accomplished.

Everybody gets an award, a medal, for participating, because that is an achievement in its own right. Then we have special awards. We honor the most improved players, usually two in each group; the "best team player," or the kid who's not a great star but a real contributor; the "hardest worker," the same kind of player who is a better athlete; the best defensive and offensive players; a most valuable player; the best pitcher; and six all-stars in each division.

The parents all love the ceremony, and the kids enjoy the honors. It's a fitting way to end a hard and fun week of camp.

I'm very passionate about teaching baseball, and so are my instructors. So if we see a little uncertainty or anxiety, we try to get it right for the players. The game is too much fun not to be contagious, and I think our appreciation rubs off.

The Decision

After I got hurt and recovered, I went to spring training with the Oakland A's, who had drafted me. That was the year, 1978, that the A's owner, Charlie Finley, tried to trade the great lefty Vida Blue to the Cincinnati Reds but was overruled by the commissioner of baseball, Bowie Kuhn. There was more than a little animosity between them.

In March, Finley was able to trade Blue to the Giants for eight players, cash, and a player to be named later. Two of the new players were catchers, and the A's wound up with too many players and, tough for me, too many catchers. So I was given my release by the A's, and it seemed that maybe "the dream" had died the day I got hurt in Chattanooga, Tennessee.

I went home to New York. I was heartbroken. What I had dreamed about my whole life seemed to be crushed, even though my shoulder was healed. It is something that many players experience, but don't want to see that day come around. I remember going home on the plane thinking, "What now?" I got home and started selling jewelry for a friend, Joe Garritti. I was doing well because I was a survivor, and I knew I needed to make some money. I was enjoying it and learning a trade that would stay with me.

Then the Yankees called. They needed a bull pen catcher, would I be interested? Of course! They were my hometown team, and the Yanks were very good. Willie Randolph, whom I'd known since Parade Ground days in Brooklyn, played second base. Thurman Munson was behind the plate, Reggie Jackson in right field, Lou Piniella in left, Mickey Rivers in center, Graig Nettles at third base, Chris Chambliss at first, Bucky Dent at short, Roy White, and Paul Blair. On the mound stood starters Catfish Hunter, Ron Guidry, and Ed Figueroa. In the bull pen, where I'd be catching them, sat All-Stars Goose Gossage, Sparky Lyle, and Don Gullett.

Free agency had just started in 1976, and the Yankees took advantage of their pocketbook.

I spoke to Bill Bergesch, who was the head of the minor-league system. We talked about me playing if something opened up in the minors, but for now he needed me in the bull pen. He told me to go down to the clubhouse and see the legendary Pete Sheehy, the Yankees' equipment manager since the days of Babe Ruth. I saw Pete, and he gave me a uniform. Could you imagine? I was in pinstripes, everybody's dream. My first number was 69.

Art Fowler, the pitching coach, then said to me in his Southern drawl, "Hey, son, come on out to the bull pen with me."

I walked out on the field at Yankee Stadium, looked up at the crowd, and got goose bumps. This is when I realized, "How cool is this?" From the minors to the majors in one month.

My test was to catch Dick "Dirt" Tidrow. They said if I could catch him, I could catch any Yankee pitcher. Why? Because he was nasty. Today, they call it filthy stuff. And he was nasty. But I was flawless. I always had good hands behind the plate.

After the first few days, Pete said, "Dom, let's get you a respectable number."

He came out with 51. It was still a high number, but Goose Gossage was 54, so I felt I came in under him, and he was a star.

"I'll take it," I said. Today, 51 is my number at Adelphi University. It has become a lucky number for me through the years.

1978 was a terrific year. There were a lot of theatrics with the manager merry-go-round. The Yankees won a hundred games, and most important a division tiebreaker against the Red Sox, when Bucky Dent hit his famous home run. We went on to win the World Series against the Dodgers, four games to two. It was an unbelievable atmosphere, made even better when I was fitted for a World Series ring.

I went back to spring training in February, ready to make the team. But there was Thurman Munson in front of me at catcher, and as an All-Star, he wasn't going anywhere. (Tragically, though, he was killed that summer when he crashed in his small plane.) Instead of going back to New York with the big club, I was looking at starting all over again in the minors.

I talked with a number of guys, including Reggie Jackson, Goose Gossage, and Willie Randolph, and they convinced me that it might be better to stay in the bull pen, stay with the Yankees, and set my sights on coaching. I could learn from some greats. I had advice from perennial All-Star catchers Elston Howard and Yogi Berra, a Hall of Famer, both coaching for the Yankees. There were an awful lot of good people around me.

So I decided to take up coaching and stayed with the Yankees for nine years. It was almost unheard of to stay with the Yankees that long. But I worked hard, and I was liked by the managers, as well as by mercurial owner George Steinbrenner. After the Yankees, I worked for Syd Thrift and the Pittsburgh Pirates as an advance scout.

It had been a fork in the road, and I have no regrets about taking it. I love coaching and giving the game back to all the kids who take that great baseball path after me. I learned so much from all the great managers and coaches through the years. The credibility that I have from being with the Yankees and Pirates is so overwhelming and gratifying that words cannot explain it.

But nothing comes easy. I worked hard for my reputation, and I try to instill this ethic in my players and campers: whatever you do, you must give 100 percent. If you do that, people will recognize it, and you will be rewarded. I will always be grateful to George Steinbrenner and Syd Thrift for giving me the opportunity to make my way in major league baseball for 13 years.

4
Advice for Coaches

Most of what I'm talking about in this book is advice for coaches, but aside from teaching and coaching baseball itself, coaches have a lot of other responsibilities. The most important responsibility is that they have charge of young people for an important part of their lives and can have a great influence on them. They can teach a lot of life lessons kids don't necessarily get in the classroom. Good sportsmanship should be at the top of the list. If sport breeds character, and I believe it does, learning to play the game with respect for your opponent is a key element. You're not going to be respected by many people if you are perceived to be a poor sport. That means grace when winning or losing.

I was lucky to have had some great coaches in my life, from Nick Marino in Catholic Youth Organization leagues to Brother Robert Kent at St. Francis Preparatory School to Jack Kaiser at St. John's University. I feel that each of them contributed to the man I am today. So always bear in mind that young minds absorb a lot, sometimes not what we wish they would (such as hitting the cutoff man), but not a lot escapes them. They don't forget the youth league coach who lost his temper and ranted and raved like a madman.

There are a lot of rewards in coaching young people. Being around kids reminds us of when we were kids. You get to see the delight in kids' faces when they do something great, or something they didn't think they could do. If you coach for a while, you can see your guys progress and come back to you and yell, "Hey, Coach, how's it going?" and stop and talk. It's a great feeling. In amateur baseball, there usually isn't any money, but you couldn't buy what you get from being a mentor to a lot of kids.

Responsibilities

That said, if you are a first-time coach there is a lot of work that you may not have expected. You may be the manager, but you can also be the grounds-keeping crew, the equipment manager, the trainer, the scheduler, and the child psychologist.

The Field

Coaches have to make sure the field is in good shape before practice and home games. Some youth programs are pretty good about doing this for you, others are not so good. Many coaches may have to rake out rough spots, groom the pitcher's mound, and repair the divots around the plate. They may have to water the field to keep the dust down. They should be familiar with bumps and other potential obstacles in the outfield, at least on their home field.

Equipment

Coaches have to make sure they have enough usable baseballs and protect the precious game balls (make sure your team knows when it needs to track down foul balls in the game and get kids hustling after them). You have to manage the bats and make sure the helmets are sound and there are enough that fit your players. Catcher's equipment tends to break at bad times, so be prepared with spare shin protectors and the means to repair your main gear. For home games, many times you are responsible for the bases, and be sure you know how to lime the baselines if it isn't done. (This is really the league president's responsibility, but what happens when everybody is ready to play and it hasn't been done? Have a phone number for this emergency, and be sure the issue is addressed in the preseason coaches' meeting.)

Scheduling

You have to get the kids there on time—for practices, for games, for pregame warm-ups, and sometimes even for parades. Which means repeating that information to them frequently, and always just as they leave: "Remember, we've got a game Saturday, 11:30 in the morning, get here at 10:00." For older kids, who may have an away game in a different town, you'll probably need to arrange a meeting point and car pool. Everybody needs as many ways to reach you as you'd like. E-mail and text messaging are great aids for the modern coach.

The Trainer

Remember, too, that kids are running around, playing, and as your father warned when you were horsing around, "somebody is going to get hurt." There are bound to be cuts, bruises, sprains, and maybe a broken bone. I can recall a time when two kids were going for a pop-up in practice, they smashed heads, and one kid left his front tooth in the other's head. For that we had to go to the hospital, but you should always have a good-size first aid kit, with cold packs for sprains. It's important to get ice on a sprain quickly to reduce swelling.

You should have at least some rudimentary first aid knowledge. When a kid gets hurt, go see what's wrong. I've seen kids writhing on the ground in obvious pain and the coach still standing on the bench watching. Get out there and try to find out what's wrong. A lot of times, it's just a bad bump on the head, or maybe he has the wind knocked out of him, so the player recovers quickly. He wants to play and he can shake it off, but he still needs a little help, a little caring, from an adult. Another great thing to know, if possible, is which child has a parent who is a medical professional and is likely to attend games. Ask the parent if you can call on him or her. You probably won't have to, because if any medical personnel are there and needed, they'll take the initiative and be on the field with you.

In Their Heads

Finally, coaches have to understand their players.

Kids really haven't figured themselves out yet. A lot of things scare them, and they are not sure what they can do yet, even though most of them can accomplish a lot more than they think. That said, some can't, and some can't do half of what they think they can. The point is they don't really know. And the adults around them may not either. So be open to possibilities and see what develops.

Now, let's separate the players into age groups.

Kids Six, Seven, and Eight

At the real young age, we're not going to dedicate a lot of time to stretching. Limber up some, but you want to make sure the kids spend a lot time catching the ball at this age. You want to make sure you have defensive drills, along with offensive drills. A lot of coaches only have an hour, an hour and a half for practice on the field. Maybe that's all they're allotted, maybe it's tough to get and keep the kids for much more than that, with all their other commitments. So the coaches go straight to hitting. Now, pretty soon, everybody can hit, but nobody can catch a ball. You have to move sometimes to the defensive end of it. I have coached young teams outside of camp, and we emphasized defense, and that's what made us winners. We were able to play defense, throw the ball and catch it. We could do cutoffs and relays. We were backing up plays. We won games that way. Nobody else was doing it.

At first, a lot of young kids playing the outfield will catch balls hit to them. But they don't know where to go with the ball.

So in our camps we do drills.

The exercise is to teach the kids that if the ball is hit to the out-field, they can't run it in and they can't hold it. With the young kids, we tell them to throw it to the nearest guy. We've found that the kids, six, seven, eight years old don't get to do this much in practice on their regular teams. We want them to know that when the ball is hit to the outfield, they must get it in as soon as possible because that prevents the runner from going from first base to second base, or second to third. They must throw it in to prevent the runner from advancing.

Fundamentals. Isn't that what they try to do to win games in the major leagues? Keep the runners from advancing and out of scoring position.

We try to do these basics a lot at our camps, and kids understand after a bit. The repetition is what teaches them. Cutoffs and relays should be done at all levels, but at each successive level they are done in a little more detail.

That advice itself is worth the price of this book. A lot of beginning coaches may not spend enough time on infield/outfield practice. You can't just have batting practice and some infield. The kids should be taught situations from the very beginning. You put players in the outfield, and you have a cutoff man. You show them how to do it. And repeat it. Repetition is simply the key to success at every level. This is why we stress relays and cutoffs in our camps at least three times a week. I guarantee that if you go over these fundamentals each practice you will see a big improvement in your team's performance come game time.

Then, when during a game somebody hits a ball out to a player, he responds as he was told: he picks the ball up and throws it right away to the next guy. Following through on what you taught him in the field will make him just as proud of himself as he would be if he got a base hit.

And he should be.

The Older Guys

With the little kids, the primary goal is to get them to throw the ball to the next closest guy and then have him throw it to the base. At the next level it's done a little faster. You teach the team where to go with the cutoffs if, for instance, the ball is hit into the gaps somewhere. We do it in college, too; we practice cutoffs and relays. As a matter of fact, here's a college kid in one of our recent games: The second baseman didn't run down the line and get a relay on a ball hit into the right field corner. He's the designated cutoff man down the line, but he stayed in his position. It was a critical, fundamental mistake, and the runner scored because of it. The ball had to be thrown all the way in to the first baseman, who was the second cutoff man. Double cutoffs are taught a little bit more in high school.

Kids may not always enjoy these drills, but when it's game time and they discover they're a well-oiled machine, they come to appreciate it.

Sometimes you have younger kids that understand a little bit more about the game, and you can teach them ahead of schedule. Don't be too rigid. Coaches have to understand their players. They need to know not only their physical capabilities, but their mental abilities, too. For instance, maybe the second baseman would ordinarily take a cutoff throw from the outfield, but he doesn't have the arm of the shortstop. So you have to devise a method so that the shortstop is always going to take the cutoff, and the second baseman is always going to cover the bag. You can do that when you have a better athlete.

Sometimes I look for that edge in college. For example, say my team has a right-hand hitter up with a man on first and third, and it looks like the other team's second baseman doesn't have a strong arm. As that situation calls for the second baseman to cover the bag on a double steal, we may be more inclined to try it, to see if we can't steal home on his weak throwing arm. That is just one of the little things that can come into play.

As for your kids' mental abilities, I'm talking more about their baseball IQ. Some of the little guys can move up because they understand the game. You can teach them more, expect more from them, and generally count on them as team leaders. There are other kids that just need a little encouragement to blossom. Maybe nobody ever had any faith in them before. It's amazing how some kids just explode given an equal chance. So get to know your guys.

Umpires

With umpires, I have a pretty good approach when I go out there. I don't consider myself an arguer. There are some guys, and I've seen it even in college, who will go out and question every little thing. It's similar to when you keep hammering somebody. Let's say, in life, someone is a negative person. He's always saying negative things. Well, after a while, people are not going to hear it anymore, they're not going to pay any attention to him.

I think that as a coach, you have to let the kids play. If you have a question with the youth league umpire, you have to understand that a lot of these umpires are instructed not to take anything, and right away, they'll say, "I don't want to hear it anymore." It can be frustrating. I've been there too. I've just asked the ump something, a mild question, and he takes it a different way. Some have attitudes, and you're not going to win with those guys once they start down that path.

My advice is, first of all, if you are going to argue something, know what the rule is. Second, I don't think you can hammer an umpire all game. It's not to anybody's advantage. You have to pick and choose your spots: for instance, a critical time, an obvious play, something like that. Finally, especially with young kids, you don't want to distract the team. Kids can easily be distracted. I have seen many cases where kids get very upset and emotional after watching adults argue. So be careful and always have the kids' best interest in mind.

Dealing with Parents

My posture is that if you are a parent and you have a question with a coach, do not bring it up during or right after a game, because there's a lot of emotion going on then. I've always had a rule: "Go home, relax, call me, and we'll talk about it." You don't have to agree with me, but you have to respect my decision because I'm the manager, I'm the coach.

Everybody looks at his own kid in a different light. Little League is supposed to be where everybody plays, because as you go up the ladder, it gets worse. Once you get to high school, the best players are playing. In the younger leagues, all the kids are supposed to be playing.

I've heard parents say, "Well, my kid is better than that kid," and this, that, and the other thing. But there could be other factors involved as to why a coach is not playing their son at that particular time. They don't know what it is. So my advice to parents is, if they have a question—and I have an open-door policy for parents at Adelphi University—they can e-mail me or call me. I just ask that you respect the manager.

Usually most coaches have a good idea why they're not playing somebody. Maybe the player is missing practice a lot. Maybe a kid doesn't pay attention when he's sitting on the bench. Maybe he doesn't pay attention when he's on the field. Maybe he's just not good enough. There are a lot of factors.

Some Often-Misunderstood Rules

Like the coaches, the umpires in much of youth league play are pretty inexperienced. So there are a few rules that everybody gets confused about. They're really pretty simple, but for some reason, some misconceptions keep getting passed down from one generation to the next. It's actually pretty funny to hear a player yelling out the same wrong thing I heard as a kid myself. I'm just going to mention a couple.

Infield Fly Rule

The first is the infield fly rule. I've seen high school games where neither the umpires nor the coaches recognized it, and to me, that's a little baffling. Just as the umpire needs to know where to run to cover every play as it develops, he should also note the situation before every pitch where the infield fly rule might apply. Like a coach, to do his job well an umpire needs to be ready for any eventuality.

So, if there are less than two outs, and runners on first and second or the bases are loaded, and the batter hits a fair pop-up that an infielder can routinely handle—the batter is out. Runners advance at their own risk. (They have to touch up if the ball is caught, but there is no force.) That's it. It's simple if you break it down into the number of outs (zero or one) and the two (just two) runners-on-base situations. The ball has to be a fair ball. Of course, catching pop-ups is no given in Little League, but it's a good rule there, too, because of why it's a rule in the first place: so that an infielder can't intentionally miss the ball and get a double play. Kids need to learn the rules early, anyway, and it's not good for them to be unfamiliar with this rule if you want to teach them how to run the bases.

The umpire should immediately step from behind the plate (or if there is a base umpire, he should call it, too) and wave his hands, call "Infield fly; batter is out," and signal an out. If he doesn't, remind him. He knows the rule; he just missed the circumstances. I've seen more confusion over this than just about anything other than the next one.

Out of Play

An errant throw goes out of play—it happens all the time, at every level, but it's much more common with younger kids. The penalty according to the rule book is "two bases," but it depends on where the runners are when the errant throw occurs. Some people say it's "the base the runner was going to, plus one," and then they add the reasoning that if the runner was returning to the last base he touched that counts as the first base. Well, no. If the fielding team throws it out of play, the runner gets the next base after the last base he passed, and one more base (two bases, the explanation almost leads to the confusion).

For instance, a runner is on first and the batter hits a single to the outfield. The runner rounds second base and the shortstop, who has taken the relay, sees the batter way around first and fires an errant throw in an attempt to catch him off the base. The first sacker misses it and the ball rolls out of play. The umpire rules that the runner scores and the batter goes to third, no matter whether he was trying to get back to first or not. If it had originally been a ball hit to the shortstop, and his errant throw was simply to get the batter at first, then the runners are at second and third, because the batter started at home, his last base.

Another occasional misconception is the wild pitch or passed ball that rolls out of play, mostly at youth league fields with just a backstop. Runners get one base on a pitched ball. If they were steal-ing at the time, it doesn't matter. That's one steal that won't go on the stat sheet.

Once Again, It's Fundamental

One of the problems in youth league baseball is that most of the coaches are volunteers, they're usually somebody's father or some-thing, and they have limited experience playing. Every once in a while, you'll catch a guy who played college ball or good high school ball. But from what I've noticed recently, for the most part, you don't get that today. As a result, many coaches don't know the basic fun-damentals of the game, and they don't go over them. I really believe that it's very important that you do, and it's the most valuable thing you can pass on to your players, beyond any trophies or year-end awards. The younger players are when they can figure these things out, the easier it's going to be for them as they get older, and ulti-mately those kids are going to be better ballplayers as a result.

Another big fundamental that today's coaches often do not understand—and it is critical—is that the coach should always remind kids during a game of the situation. For example, with run-ners at first and second base, the coach should remind each player who could determine the outcome of the next play what he needs to do. In this case, the coach would say, "If it's hit to third, step on third and go to first. If it's hit to second, go to the shortstop at second for the force play. If it's back to the pitcher, go to second for the double play." Make it fresh in their minds before the play happens. I guar-antee they will react faster and with better judgment.

Remember, do not assume they know what to do! Tell them before it happens.

In our One-on-One Baseball camps, we try to prepare the kids for the next level. What happens is this: Many high schools that are popular for baseball get up to 200 kids trying out for their fresh-man teams. All these kids are coming out, and they were average to above-average players when they played on their grammar school and youth league teams. But as you go up the pyramid, the compe-tition gets narrower. Many parents say, "You ought to see him hit," but the coach has 200 kids, and he doesn't have room on his roster for 200 kids. So a player had better be fundamentally sound in all aspects of the game.

The first cuts, right off the bat, and it's probably half the kids, are kids that can't throw properly, or can't catch the ball properly, or can't field a ground ball properly, or, most important, those kids who simply are not instinctively baseball people. In other words, when the coach hits a fungo, where does the player go? If a player is one of those kids who is not prepared early, he could be in trouble.

Let's say the prospective player is a shortstop, and the coach hits a fungo to the outfield, and he sees that the shortstop doesn't know where to go for a cutoff. Well, that guy is going to be in jeopardy, because the coach may not have the time to teach and develop at this level. A player shouldn't have to be taught that in high school. That's what separates the high school player from the regular player. That's how players get cut from teams right off the bat. When there are 100 to 200 players trying out, the coach is going to say, "Well, I'm not going to have time to teach this kid where he has to go to get a cutoff, because he's never going to get it now."

If he sees a kid go to field a ground ball and he sees the kid come in and try to one-hand the ball, rather than get in front of it and set up, that kid is not going to make the team either.

That's why we try to teach the kids the basic fundamentals of the game, so that when they get to the next level, they understand them. They look like ballplayers.

Is it important that grammar school kids go to summer camps and get outside instruction? Well, that's why we do it. I believe that we give them more bang for their buck. They get more than their parents' money's worth. We are sincere and we are passionate about what we want to teach the kids. That's why we have a plan every day. Otherwise, we'd be babysitters. That's why we get upset if we have a couple of kids that horse around and hurt the balance of the day. It takes a little discipline to learn the fundamentals, and why miss the fun of doing it right?

The Player's Wife: Yolanda

Since Dom was little, he had that dream of being a professional baseball player.

Then in one day it was gone. It was heartbreaking. He really took it on the chin.

But he eventually found what he's really good at: teaching baseball, as opposed to just playing it. He's very hands-on. Sometimes people go to other camps, they come back here, and they say the same thing. "Most people whose names appear on the other camps' brochures aren't there. You don't see them with the kids. They're administrative."

Dom is out there with the kids, playing with them, getting in the dirt with them. He can tell you every kid's name, who hit what, especially the kids that come back year after year. He can tell you what little Johnny did a couple summers ago and how he's coming along. He's got a great rapport with them. Look at who's out there helping run the camp, all his college players and past players. They flock back to him, because he's just that genuine.

I really feel this is his niche in life. He found his real calling, even though he didn't get the one he initially wanted. He feels comfortable teaching the kids and really cares that they get it. He wants them to understand what it takes to get to their dream.

We met when he came back from Maryland. It became a joke for us. We met the week after he came back from giving up his football scholarship at Maryland. He wouldn't take me to meet his dad, because he was afraid his father would think he left Maryland to come back to me. I didn't even know him before he went away to school. But the timing was so close. His father thought he was going to be this big football star.

I've known Dom since he played baseball at St. John's. I pretty much went through all of it: I was with him the whole four years at St. John's, when he was drafted by the Oakland A's, the shoulder injury, when he was released after his injury, going to the Yankees, all of that stuff.

It's been something. We've lived in cycles.

When he was with the Yankees, Dom used to do camps with the Dave Winfield foundation. When he left the Yankees, he did camps with the Mets organization. He got involved because, as president of the Our Lady of Hope Athletic Association, he rented the field to the Mets for their camps. So when he talked to the Mets representative to rent the field, the Mets man said to Dom, "Oh, do you want to work?" Dom became an instructor in the baseball camp for a year. It was run so poorly, he said, "I can do this. I can do this better."

So the next year, we did one week, then two weeks, and once he went to Adelphi, we did camps in Long Island, and then we added a high school camp for a fifth week. Now we're up to seven weeks a summer. And when you read this book we will be all year round, indoors and outdoors.

He got four notes just yesterday from little kids who went to camp a couple weeks ago that said, "I loved your camp. I'm coming back."

Another longtime camper, Rob, sent a picture from a fundraiser that Dom was at with Goose Gossage and Lee Mazzilli. His mother wrote a note saying, "You always make my son feel so special." Dom took the time to introduce him and let him meet each player. One was, of course, the newest member of the Hall of Fame, Goose Gossage. His mother told me Rob couldn't sleep that night. That's just the way Dom is.

I thought for him the injury would be devastating; but he found a new dream, and I think that has been fulfilled.

5
Athleticism

L et's take a brief break to talk about athleticism. I use
the term all the time, but I'm not talking just about
the natural, extremely gifted athletes who can walk
out on the field and throw a 90-mph strike from the first day.
All players have the ability to use athleticism to their advantage, to learn to use it, to practice and develop it until it's
second nature.

Some people are born to be athletes, but some people
have to work at it. Some people are just natural ballplayers:
they can see the ball, they can feel the ball, they know where
it's coming off the bat instinctively, they recognize pitches
from the spin of the ball, they have great hand-eye coordination. Another bunch of players work their tails off to get

to the place their more gifted teammates arrived at a long time before. These guys develop themselves into athletes. Of course, the naturals have to work at it too, if they want to get better. No matter how good a player is, chances are, at the next level, he's going to have to improve just to compete.

Among the things players can do to improve, if they're in either group, include agility and karaoke drills. If players work at these specific drills and exercise them, they'll give themselves a little more of the athlete's grace. Moving like an athlete brings all the other elements of the game to a player, and players can get much better at it with practice.

Way to Go Boom!

Baseball is a game of explosiveness. When a player is on first base, he explodes to steal second. When he puts the ball in play, he's exploding out of the box. When he plays the outfield, he's exploding toward where the ball is hit. When he's the shortstop and the ball is hit in the hole, his first two steps are so important as to whether he'll get the out. Baseball is not so much a game of speed as it is a game of quickness.

Players have to be quick to get to the baseball in the hole, to get out of the box, to get a good jump on a fly ball. It's quickness, hand speed, bat speed; everything has to be done quicker and faster as players go up the ladder. You can look at all the different aspects of the game and find the quickness factor. There's the quickness of the pitcher's move to first. The "boom-boom" plays at any base. Umpires use the sound of the ball hitting the glove to determine if a runner is safe at first because they must look at the base for the runner's foot. Baseball is much more a game of inches than football is, despite its measuring chain.

Agility in baseball is becoming just as important as brawn. Agility workouts are just as important as batting and pitching lessons. Many players today are going to the local training center to make sure they are getting every edge possible. I recommend that they start at age 12; at this age, their bodies are starting to develop and can withstand the pounding of these vigorous workouts.

Some Real-Life Examples

The Alex Rodriguezes of the world are born with it, but look at little David Eckstein. He's a tremendous catalyst on every team he plays on. He's a workhorse with seemingly less than major league skills. Yet he has two World Series rings with two different teams. Right now, A-Rod has none. Now, one player doesn't have control of the play that gets his team a World Series trophy, as anyone can parade around a partying clubhouse, but some guys seem to help team chemistry. A-Rod has won three MVP awards. The only MVP award Eckstein has won was the one they doled out for the guy who best helped his team win the 2006 World Series. Alex is clearly the better athlete, a certain Hall of Fame entrant on the first ballot, and his numbers put him up there with the greatest hitters of all time. So who knows which way fate takes you, but Eckstein is an example of a guy whose work ethic and passion make him a winner.

There have been hundreds of major league ballplayers who aren't superior born athletes: for instance, Lenny Dykstra, the great Mets and Phillies catalyst, and Craig Counsell, a lifetime .255 hitter with two World Series rings, a championship MVP, and some key bloop hits that won decisive games. Brooks Robinson was always a good fielder, but a spectacular 1970 World Series helped get him into the Hall with only a .267 lifetime average. Who can forget Bucky Dent's famous blast? Or Bill Mazeroski's "shot heard 'round the world" in the 1960 World Series?

David Wright, the great young third baseman for the Mets, doesn't look like he can run. He's a stocky guy, but he has worked on his quickness. He was a good player in the minor leagues, but he made himself a better player. He runs hard and steals a lot of bases, especially for a third baseman; he increased his stolen-base total in each of his first three years in the majors. He goes from first to third as well as just about anybody.

I saw Greg Maddux when he came up with the Cubs. I was the advance scout for the Pirates at the time. He was a little guy but real smart, a great fielder ("very athletic," I wrote in my report back then) with a good sinker, slider, and changeup. His fastball wasn't overwhelming, but he'd throw down and in, down and away, and then he'd throw a little slider, and then he'd take something off. He became a great pitcher. He was only about 170 pounds. Maddux has a lot of God-given ability, but he was still playing at age 42 and still winning games because he's smart and he works at it. He didn't win 18 Gold Gloves because he thought that all he had to do on the mound was pitch. He knows where to be and where to throw the ball. Always.

Maddux studies every pitch of the game. His catcher with the Braves, Eddie Perez, tells a story of Maddux intentionally throwing an inside fastball to Jeff Bagwell in a game that the Braves were winning 8–0, knowing that Bagwell would hit it out and cost Maddux his shutout. Perez didn't understand, but Maddux explained to Perez that the Braves would probably be seeing the Astros in the playoffs, and Bagwell would be looking for that same pitch because he had hit it for a home run. Sure enough, two months later the Braves met the Astros, and Bagwell kept sitting on a pitch he never got, waiting for that inside fastball while Maddux struck him out away, away, away.

Rick Ankiel had a lot of natural talent, and he was such a rookie phenom, with a booming curve, that he was put into Game 1 of the National League playoffs in 2000—and suddenly lost his ability to throw strikes, or even find the catcher's mitt. It was a mental condition that has doomed many a major leaguer, but none of them have gone back to the minor leagues and worked their way back to the majors, to everyday jobs patrolling center field and hitting home runs, as he has. Babe Ruth did pitch for the Red Sox before becoming an everyday player, but the Babe, a fine pitcher, didn't give it up because he was wild—at least on the mound.

All these guys are major leaguers and examples of how even great ballplayers need to work at the game every day, all year round. They have to.

We have to mention one more guy, who just about epitomizes the player who makes himself better—Derek Jeter. When he was younger he was thin and he was fast. But you watch him run now and he runs hard, has a perfect way of running. He is a natural talent, but he still got better. He's a guy who never quits, either. He was hitting only .190 at the end of May in 2004, and the New York press was horrified, but he ended the year at almost .300 as usual, playing great shortstop.

The Will Is the Way

The first thing in the spring is to identify and work on players' weaknesses. And the best thing players can do for themselves if they need help identifying their own weaknesses is to ask their coach. As a coach, one of your first jobs is to identify all your players' strengths and weaknesses so you can address them and help them improve.

For instance, say I've got a third baseman on my team, a big strong kid, about 225 pounds, who has good hands and works hard on the field to get better, but there's one thing he doesn't do well—he doesn't get out of the box as fast as he should. One simple thing I would tell this kid to do would be to run 10 to 15 hard sprints a day, from the athletic position, as if he were going to steal a base.

The "athletic position"—this is one of my favorite phrases; example: "Hey, Ryan, get a little more athletic in your stance." "Bobby, get more athletic when you field a ground ball." You'll hear this a lot from me at my camps. If you think about it, you *always* have to be in an athletic position—hitting, fielding, pitching, running, catching, and throwing.

In training, players have to tell themselves when they're running to move their legs faster. A lot of people don't realize that, but in order to get better, players have to believe they can actually will themselves to run faster.

If a player wants to be a better hitter, he has to tell himself, "I want to hit the ball to right center." So he has to put that right-center swing on it. Let's say that a pitcher has been trying to throw the player inside. What he wants to do is try to open up faster, he has to look for it. He tells himself, "turn on the ball, I want to hit the ball a little more in front of the plate in that situation."

It's the same thing in running. If a player is on first base, he has to tell himself, "Okay, I really want to run hard here." And he has to turn those legs as fast as he can. Now, I know some people will say, "Yeah, but a player can only do as much as he can." That's not true. If a player tells his feet to get faster, he's going to get faster.

Drills

At One-on-One Baseball, we do agility drills twice a week. This is only an introduction, but it gives the kids the idea that you have to improve in other aspects besides hitting and throwing in order to improve in baseball.

We like karaoke, ladder, cones, jump rope, circle, and hurdle drills. Karaoke drills are especially great for quickness. Have the players start out a little slow to get a feel for it. They should start in an athletic position, on their toes. They don't have to take long strides. To get quicker, they should do it quicker. Have them do it 10 times, and it'll make them quicker each time.

Of course, you can also do side-to-side running, where the players simply move sideways, propelling one leg after the other; or the ice-skating drill, where players move forward as if they were sliding along on skates like you see in Olympic speed skating. Have the players try to get faster and faster as they get more comfortable with the motion. They should tell their feet to get quicker and quicker.

Another good quickness drill is for players to practice sprints as if they were stealing a base. Have them start in the athletic position. They should not start to run standing up; a lot of kids stand straight up right away. No good! Tell them to stay down and go.

The cone drills are good agility drills. Position cones in an obstacle course fashion and have the players run around them, cutting them close, or use any of the karaoke movements. Mix it up.

You can do any number of things with the feet in ladder drills; all you need is an agility ladder laid on the ground, or tape a ladder shape if you're inside in a gym in bad weather. Vary how the players move through the ladder. It can be a little like hopscotch.

We also use a "jump box," a box one to two feet high that players jump on and off of.

We set these drills up in stations, so that the players are getting a good workout and using different parts of their muscles as they negotiate each station. Again, repetition is the key in building muscle memory. Jumping rope is also good.

Stretching

We stretch every day when we're out on the field. But make sure your players warm their muscles up a little bit before they start to stretch them. We always take a jog around the field before we stretch.

Karaoke

If you've watched a quarterback drop back to pass, you've seen a karaoke drill. Basically the players are moving sideways; their chest is facing one way and their legs are propelling them another. First, they cross their left leg over their right and move laterally; their hips will swivel. Then they stride with a scissors-like step with their right leg laterally but behind their left leg. Then they cross their left leg behind the right and continue to move. Repeat to the opposite side. It's a little like learning a dance step. Have the players start slowly until they have the movements and gradually increase their speed.

Some light running gets the blood flowing and warms the muscles so that when we stretch them, we don't do more harm than good. It's similar to pulling on a cold rubber band. It's brittle. So are the tendons and muscles when they're not warmed up. You wouldn't start a locomotive without a head of steam, and kids shouldn't start working their muscles until they're ready to be worked.

Players must stretch before they begin exercise. Help them understand that they must pay attention to the muscle they're trying to stretch, so they can really figure out how far they can stretch that muscle. They shouldn't just stretch their hamstrings out for the sake of stretching them. They've got to feel the hamstring and say, "oh, I can go a little bit more and a little bit more" until right there, "let me hold that."

Assurance, Not a Strut

Have your players watch how guys who are true athletes carry themselves. They'll walk a little differently, a little more self-assured. Generally their movements are slowed down to a catlike elegance: they could go faster if they needed to, but right now, what's the rush? There's a certain relaxed tension in the arms, the legs. Have your

Stretching to avoid injury

players try it for a while. It's pretty comfortable, and will help them relax. To be athletic is to be poised and ready. It's the way our bodies really want to be, when we can chase out the worry that seems to always follow tense people around. Players should aim to be patient and assured.

In baseball, that means before each play, each and every play, players are in a ready position, on the balls of their feet and ready to move. As Yogi Berra has said, "Half of the game is 90 percent mental." A huge part of the game is how players carry themselves. Being confident that they'll make the play helps them make the play. Confidence is contagious, and if players take the time to develop an athletic bearing, they'll play better and so will the guys around them. I am not talking about arrogance, but the confidence built through a commitment to athleticism.

Gene Lamont

I've known Gene Lamont ever since I was an advance scout for the Pittsburgh Pirates and Gene was the third-base coach there. We talked all the time about the opposing teams coming in, and we became good friends. He went on to be the Manager of the Year in 1993 with the Chicago White Sox. Gene managed the White Sox for five years and the Pirates for another five years in the '90s. A former major league catcher with the Tigers, Gene, like me, traded in the "tools of ignorance" (a term coined by jokester and lawyer Herold "Muddy" Ruel, a catcher for the great Walter Johnson in the 1920s) to become a coach and show other guys how to play the game of baseball. A lot of managers are ex-catchers, probably because catchers manage the game from behind the plate, calling pitches, positioning fielders, often even controlling the tempo. You have to really know the game to be a good catcher.

Gene offers these tips to young people learning the game and their coaches.

On Improving Your Swing

A lot of kids have a natural uppercut, so you need to work on a nice level swing. We all tend to uppercut, so hitting off a tee is a good way to even that out.

The tee has to be in the proper spot. If you're practicing hitting the inside pitch you want the tee closer to you. Conversely, if you want to practice going to the opposite field, the tee needs to be set up away. If you don't move the tee, change where you stand in the box.

Soft toss is also becoming very popular, and it's good to a point, but you have to also be aware of bat speed. Get out on the field sometimes when you play soft toss, instead of hitting from inside the cages. You can get a much better idea of how you are hitting the ball if it's not just crashing into the screen. All the best hitters have good bat speed, so bat speed is very important. Everything can seem to be hit pretty hard in the cage, that's why you need to judge it out on the field.

On Baserunning

Baserunning is the hardest thing to practice. You can't practice base stealing. You can practice running the bases, rounding corners, hitting the bags, but it's hard to simulate stealing. The best thing to do is to put yourself on first base during batting practice and work on getting a jump. Running fast is one thing, but the mental part is harder to practice.

If you're a coach, have your guys out there on the bases during batting practice. And running hard, 100 percent. Just going at 75 percent speed doesn't cut it. You don't get anything out of that.

You can be a really good runner, without necessarily being fast. The secret is in anticipation. That's how you get a good jump. It determines whether you can take off if the ball goes into the dirt. If you're not thinking ahead, not anticipating, you're going to miss it and not get a jump. It's hard to simulate, unless you put a man on first base and you throw a number of pitches, with one every now and then getting into the dirt.

On Throwing the Ball

Get the kids to go out and just play, not everything has to be practice. Let them do things on their own. One thing that I think is wrong today is that kids don't throw very well, and that's because they don't go outside and play a little when they're not at practice. My dad always played catch with me, and I think that's important.

The kids can have a lot of fun in the sandlots, like we used to do as kids. There needs to be a change in the culture of kids' play, maybe, but let them play a little disorganized baseball.

I think things have become almost too organized. Kids need to play catch with each other, with just themselves. They don't need to be pitching, just throwing the ball back and forth. It makes for better hands, better arms. They can practice by aiming the ball at the other guy's head or belt if he doesn't catch it. (Obviously, they aren't trying to actually hit their partner in the head with the ball—he's supposed to catch it there.) Make a game of it, 5 points for the belt, 25 points for a head shot, or make up your own rules. Anytime you can make a game out of it, it's that much more fun, just like it is in golf.

A catcher can practice hitting the other guy in the shoulder. There's nothing worse for a pitcher than to have to work to get throws back from his catcher.

You can make yourself a better thrower with practice. One of the guys I saw make the most improvement as a thrower was Barry Bonds. When I was with the Pirates, he and Bobby Bonilla used to play long toss every day. You stretch that arm out. They're throwing 250 feet or so, not line drives, just good hard throws, stretching the arm out. It definitely made Barry a much better thrower.

You have to throw properly, working at 100 percent. Fielding just 15 ground balls a day also makes a difference.

On Playing the Game

You just can't develop bad habits. It can be very hard, if not impossible to unlearn them.

The most important thing is to play the game. There is nothing better for a guy trying to make the big leagues than getting four at bats a game in the minor leagues, getting three or four balls hit to him in a game. This is true at any age. You really can't simulate what it's like in a game. Only a game does that.

Finally, I think parents put an awful lot of pressure on kids, and it makes life tougher on them. They need to have fun, without all the pressure.

6
Keeping It Simple: Pitching

The pitcher's job is to get outs. Even the great strikeout pitcher Sandy Koufax, who has the highest career winning percentage in the major leagues (165–87, .655), said that he was primarily interested in getting the batter out. In youth leagues, a lot of outs will come with strikeouts, but that's more a question of matchups than anything else. To get outs, the successful pitcher throws strikes. Staying around the plate is the most effective thing a young pitcher can do.

Consistent strikes, pitches that can result in the ball being put in play at any point, keep teammates in the field focused. If your pitcher is walking everyone, going into long counts on every batter, fielders will drift. When fielders' minds start to drift, errors, mental and otherwise, are right around the corner.

Pitchers must practice to learn control along with learning to throw hard. I can't emphasis this enough. At the same time, they need to learn the proper way to pitch—with their legs and back supplying the energy—when they are as young as possible. You don't want them to develop bad habits that become harder to break as they get older.

Teach Mechanics Early

For instance, I was watching a kid throw the other day at my 11-year-old nephew's game. I spoke to the coach on the opposing team and said, "This kid has a lot of potential."

As a coach, when I see a kid with "potential," especially a young pitcher, what I'm usually looking at is great athleticism aside from pitching talent. This kid got off the mound well. When the ball was hit he got over before it was fielded by the second baseman, and he ran over to first base to take the throw. A kid that bounces around, knows where to go is what I call an instinctive player. This is something you cannot teach. He is a player who will develop faster than others.

The pitcher I was watching threw strikes, but he had nothing on the ball, and that might have kept him below the radar of other coaches. He was throwing with just his wrist and his arm, but at age 11, that's fine. Of course, if a pitcher keeps doing it that way he's going to develop bad habits, which will need to be broken as early as possible, because sometimes it can be too late. The pitcher's muscle memory won't give up the poor mechanics.

That's why we say, "Perfect practice makes perfect." He may be a pretty good pitcher in his league now, just throwing the ball with his arm, with some guys hitting it—and they did. But if he gets his arm back and throws with his legs and back, I guarantee you that some of those guys, those mediocre guys who are hitting the ball now, will wind up swinging and missing because the ball is going to be past them before they know what to do with it. I like getting a kid like him, with good instincts but still looking for the zip on his fastball, to come to our camps, knowing that we can help him take the next step.

On the Mound

Now, let's step to the mound. Let's keep it simple with just a few basic rules.

The pitcher should begin by straddling the mound. He should not get on the rubber until he is ready to pitch. (The pitcher also can't stand on the rubber without the ball; it's a balk.) When the pitcher is ready to pitch, he should stand square on the rubber facing the plate.

Younger kids, seven or eight years old, who may not be able to get the basic windup, can start in the stretch position. Starting this way allows them to concentrate on throwing strikes without wor-

The pitcher stands square on the rubber.

rying about bringing their arms up and bringing them back. From the stretch, they are already in the most important position to throw the ball—they are balanced. They can learn the windup when they are more confident. The most important position is where they're balanced. Whether they start from the stretch position or they use the rocker step to arrive at the same position, they must be balanced to throw the ball.

If they are comfortable with the windup, have them rocker step back as they bring their arms up over their head. Then have them turn their right foot in front of the rubber. Start, rock, and come to that balanced position. They get their arm out, and then they get to the power position, where they will direct all the force generated by their legs and arm speed toward home plate.

You want to be sure to get them to that balance-point position to deliver the ball.

A good way for them to get a feel for the balance-point position is to have them get in the stretch and stand on their back leg. I have my guys do this, and while they're standing there I say, "Get bal-

The pitcher takes a rocker step back.   The balance-point position

Hands are separated.

The glove is out, the arm is back.

anced. You've got the ball in your hand? Now throw it. You should be able to throw the ball just as hard as you can doing all the other rigmarole before that." Balance is very, very important, because you get most of your strength from your legs.

As they deliver the ball, at the same time, they should separate the hands while moving forward. The glove goes out toward the plate, the arm goes back, the ball pointing toward center field.

Remember to have them keep their front side tucked in (left side for right-handers, right side for left-handed pitchers).

Wherever a pitcher's left shoulder is pointed, most of the time that's where the ball is going to go. (Of course, it's the right shoulder for a left-handed thrower.) If the pitcher opens up, the ball is going to be up and in to a right-handed batter, up and away to a left-hander. That's why the pitcher should always keep his glove side tucked in as long as he can.

I tell my kids to "stay level, your eyes at the target, the catcher's mitt, at all times. When you're breaking your hands and you're in

The glove side is tucked in.   Glove shoulder determines ball location.

the balance position, you shouldn't be tilted." There were a certain number of guys in the big leagues that could get away with starting in a tilt. I'm thinking back a few years, guys like Jim Bunning and Juan Marichal, had that big leg kick, but like everybody else, when it came time to throw the ball they were in the right position. But that's very hard to do, with normal kids.

I tell my guys at Adelphi, "Just stay quiet, stay level. Keep your shoulder and your glove side in. And boom, throw strikes.

"Keep your head still and your eyes on the target all the way through the pitch. If your eyes are on the target, then your head shouldn't move.

"Finally, come through the pitch, your glove pointed toward the ground. Always finish the pitch." A lot of guys fall apart here. They don't finish their follow-through. The arm needs to come across the body and end down. "Feel like you're putting your shoulder and your back into it. You shouldn't be standing up after you deliver the ball.

"If you follow through correctly, you should finish in an athletic/fielder's position. This is important for two reasons: one, so you are ready to field a ball hit back at you or to go get a bunt; and two, to ensure your follow-through."

The follow-through

The pitcher is a fielder too, remember. Often, with little kids, he is a pretty important fielder. So it is vital he be able to pick up ground balls and bunts and knows, ahead of time, where he is going to throw it.

If a pitcher throws a pitch and the ball is high, there's one simple thing that he didn't do. He didn't follow through. I'll tell my kids, "If you throw the next pitch, and you follow through, and you become

The athletic/fielder's position from two different angles

a fielder, I'll bet you that next ball is down." Ninety-five percent of the time it is.

"So the next time you throw a pitch and it's high, you'll know why," I tell them. This is one of the things we stress. It's just a tip, so that if something goes wrong, you can correct it.

Reaching Out

There's a lot of confusion about the term "driving" toward the plate. It's used to mean delivering the ball forward with force, but it can be misinterpreted in some pitchers' minds. Used generically, it's OK, but when you are adjusting a pitcher, it can throw him off. Instead of telling a pitcher to "drive toward" the plate, tell him to reach out with his front leg "toward" the plate. If you tell him to "drive toward" the plate as he comes down from the balance position, he is going to push off with his back, rubber foot and will rush his delivery. It will be a lot harder for him to stay back and in the balance position as he delivers the ball.

Instead, tell the young pitcher to reach toward the plate with that front leg and get as far out as he can, and then pull his front half forward with his front leg. That will keep him closed and keep his weight balanced. And when he lands, he will be in a balanced, square position.

If a pitcher is "driving," his tendency will be to push off with the back foot and leave all his weight on his front half. He will have nothing to come through with and will lose velocity. He'll be throwing with this arm instead of his legs and back, and the ball will tend to sail.

What to Throw

As to pitches, here's what I like to teach kids: fastball, changeup, three-finger changeup. I teach younger kids to throw a four-seam fastball. As we've discussed earlier, when you grip a baseball across four seams, it flies generally truer, straighter, than one gripped with just two seams. The two-seamer tends to sail, which is why a pitcher might throw it when he gets older and has better control. But with little kids, control is the biggest concern. A kid that's got a good arm and throws strikes will have plenty of success just throwing fastball strikes.

As pitchers get older you can add pitches. Most major leaguers use what's called a circle changeup, but little kids' fingers aren't long enough. So with younger kids, you show them that instead of putting two fingers on the fastball, they put three fingers, settle it back a little more in the hand, and just throw it like a regular fastball. It'll come off with the same spin and less speed. If they tuck the ball back in their hand, it will come off with a little more friction, and so it'll drop down a little bit. It's what I call choking the ball.

I don't like curveballs for young kids. I would teach them a little cutter, though, at maybe 11, 12, or 13, and as they get into high school. A little cutter is what Mariano Rivera throws (only his cutter runs in at 94 mph). A little cutter doesn't put much strain on your elbow, and Mariano has had very few injury problems. With the cutter, you're just turning your hand a little at the end of a fastball. The ball is going to move a little bit. If the hitter is seeing fastball, fastball, fastball, and then just a little movement, it's a pretty deceptive pitch. That's good enough for kids.

Care with Growing Arms

Young people haven't fully developed. Their bones, muscles, and tendons are still growing, and their joints are particularly sensitive

Four-seam fastball

Two-seam fastball

Different views of a circle change

to strain. A curveball or slider puts enormous strain on the shoulder and elbow, and the ligaments that take the brunt of the twisting motion required in the arm to throw a curve can be damaged. It may not be immediately apparent, but somewhere down the road a

Teaching kids to choke the ball as an alternative

kid could end up a candidate for the increasingly common Tommy John surgery, or ulnar collateral ligament reconstruction (UCL).

Named after the first big-league pitcher to get it, the surgery replaces a ligament in the throwing elbow with another redundant ligament, often from the other arm's wrist. It repairs the damage wrought by the stress a pitcher puts on his arm. Studies seem to indicate that overuse, too many pitches thrown, may be the biggest issue in causing this damage, but poor mechanics are also a problem.

As a coach, you have to be careful with your best young pitcher. You may be tempted to trot him out there every game because he throws strikes. But be very careful you don't ask too much of a still growing kid. Most leagues, these days, limit the number of innings a kid can pitch a week (or have similar restrictions based on pitch counts instead), but know that some kids will play in multiple leagues, not to mention the occasional pickup game on their own. A good coach will always be aware of the issue and take care of his pitching staff. Don't be afraid to ask your pitcher during an inning, "How do you feel?" Check his reaction to the question, even if he says he is fine. If you feel he is telling you the truth, stay with him. If there is hesitation, take him out.

The key thing to pay attention to, though, isn't so much innings, but his pitch count. You don't need to do elaborate pitching charts. At most sports stores, you can buy a little metal counter you hold in your hand and just punch down the counter with each pitch. It's pretty simple and mindless; you can do it and still concentrate on the game,

Pitches like the slider (left) and curveball (right) should not be taught to kids until they get to the high school level.

or you can designate another coach or parent to keep the count. The number of pitches a young athlete should throw varies by age.

At the beginning of the season, you should also increase the number of pitches a kid throws by 10 to 15 each outing. That will help build arm strength and stamina.

A Good Philosophy

The best pitching coach I've ever been around, and I've been around a lot of pitching coaches, was Ray Miller. He was with the Baltimore Orioles with manager Earl Weaver when he had four 20-game winners in 1971: Jim Palmer, Mike Cuellar, Pat Dobson, and Dave McNally. I had the honor of being with Ray when I was in Pittsburgh. He was with the Pirates when I was an advance scout there. (An advance scout usually scouts the teams ahead on the schedule of a major league team and gives advice on how to pitch players, among other things.)

Ray had a philosophy that I now instill in my guys. "Work fast. Change speeds. Throw strikes."

Your pitchers must work fast because you want to make sure you keep your guys in the game. You want them to change speeds all the time. You want to keep the hitters off-balance. And they should throw strikes, not walk guys. If a pitcher challenges hitters and doesn't walk guys, most of the time, you keep your team in the game. That's a very good philosophy to teach the older kids. If you think about it, you can do that with the little kids, too. At all levels, it will win games.

Keep this in mind: When you walk the leadoff hitter in the inning, he will score 70 percent of the time. If you walk *anyone* in the game, he will score 50 percent of the time. How's that for an interesting stat?

It doesn't have to be as sophisticated with the little kids, but get them to work fast. I'm not saying rapid-fire. Just get the ball back and be ready to pitch again. If the kids are 11, 12, or 13, they can change speeds: maybe throw one a little harder, one a little softer. And throw strikes, of course. You need that at any level.

Simple Rules for Pitchers

Straddle the mound.
Stand square on the rubber.
Take a rocker step back, turn back foot in front of rubber.
Come to the balance-point position.
Separate hands while moving forward.
Glove goes out, arm goes back.
Keep glove side tucked in.
Where the glove shoulder goes, the ball goes.
Stay level, don't tilt.
Keep your eyes on the target at all times.
Follow through, glove toward feet.
Finish in athletic/fielder's position.

Drills

The following are good drills for pitchers.

Pitchers' Fielding Practice

We call our drills PFP—pitchers' fielding practice. Because of the pitchers' unique role in baseball, they get separated from the other players a lot as we try to keep everybody busy. Pitchers have certain drills that will improve their skills and keep them sharp in between games. This is something that a coach can do during practice, at the end of practice, or as a second practice during the week. It's very important, because it can win you games.

Work on bunt plays. Make sure the pitcher throws the pitch, he gets off the mound, he knows where to go and how to get to the ball. Some kids don't know how to do that.

For instance, if a pitcher is a left-hander and the ball is hit down the third-base line, does he go where he has to turn his body around to field the ball? No, he goes with his glove side, he gets the ball, and he makes a pivot and throws.

In this drill, the fielder takes the ground ball as the pitcher covers first to receive the flip.

Follow-Through and Fielding

This drill is used to get a pitcher to follow through and end in the athletic/fielding position.

Start with the pitcher on the mound. He pitches to a catcher. The coach immediately hits a separate ball on the ground, back to the pitcher, forcing him to field the ball.

Also practice different fielding situations. Simulate them with runners on base, as you would with your infielders. Go over proper pickoff moves. Have pitchers practice working out of the stretch, both holding runners close and delivering the ball. Go through all the bunting scenarios, with the pitcher throwing the ball and landing in an athletic/fielding position.

Building Arm Strength

Pitchers should always take a day off after pitching in a game. The next day, they'll most likely be sore, so they should come out and just stretch out their arm and body. From there it's okay to have a catch and, depending on how they feel, even to start throwing a little longer, just to stretch it out a little bit. For older kids, the third day is a throw day, preparing for the next start. For all kids, have them throw a little bit at first, not hard, just to loosen up.

MEDIUM LONG TOSS. The length depends on the strength of the athlete's arm. Have them loosen up at a regular catching distance for 20 to 25 throws. Then have one player move back 50 feet for medium long toss throws (about 10 to 15 more). The players must throw harder to reach the other player. This stretches the arm muscles out and helps keep them limber.

The players should not throw the ball like a pop-up to the other guy. They should throw it more like a line drive. The throws don't have to be rapid-fire, but the players should take a crow hop to get momentum behind the ball and complete the throw with a good follow-through.

FULL LONG TOSS. For the last 10 to 15 throws, have the players back away another 100 feet. These are harder throws, with more arc. Players should do this twice a week if they're not pitching.

Throwing long is always good, no matter what age the players, just adjust the distance to the kids' strength. Older kids should be sure to do long toss three days after pitching in a game.

ROUTINE. Pitchers should follow a simple routine after games. Let's say they pitched a game on Saturday: they should take Sunday off, on Monday play catch, on Tuesday do a long toss.

Using the Legs

Players should get into the balance position and drive toward the plate holding a towel in their pitching hand. The towel provides resistance. The players' pants should bunch up on the back leg (another wrinkle effect) if their weight is properly distributed.

Use a cone in back to ensure that the back leg picks up.

Running

Pitchers need to run more than other players because so much of their velocity comes from the strength in their legs. Running builds both leg strength and the endurance they need to throw the ball on every play.

Pitchers should do both sprints and some long runs. We run what we call "poles," which is running from foul pole to foul pole along the edge of the outfield (not straight across, along the fence if there is one, an imagined fence if there isn't).

Have the pitchers do sprints one day, say ten 50-yard sprints. The day after they pitch they should do a long run, maybe a mile or two. It loosens the body up and gets the adrenaline pumping. They're not throwing, but they need to stay active.

Anything a pitcher does to build his lung capacity means that much more oxygen will be taken in when he takes a deep breath on the mound. Deep breaths on the mound are a great way for a pitcher to calm down when he has lost the strike zone.

John Franco

John Franco is *major league baseball's all-time saves leader among left-handers, and he is third among pitchers all-time in games played, with appearances in 1,119 games. In 21 seasons, he amassed 424 saves in 1,245⅔ innings. A four-time All-Star, Franco was the National League saves leader three years, and he had eight 30-save seasons. A New York native and St. John's alumnus, he was traded back home from the Cincinnati Reds to the Mets in 1990. He helped the Metropolitans in five post-season series, where he pitched in 15 games, with an ERA of just 1.88, with two wins and a save. He lives in Staten Island and coaches his son's travel team for the Richmond County Youth Organization. He's been able to coach his son since he was 14, for three years now.*

John and I have been friends since his days with the Cincinnati Reds. I was scouting for the Pittsburgh Pirates then, and one night after a game, we saw each other and went out for a drink. John, of course, went to St. John's as I did, and as former Redmen (the nickname has since been changed to the Red Storm), we had a common bond. That's one of the things about baseball: It's sort of a fraternity. We've all been through the same things; it's easy to strike up a conversation. John and I had a lot in common: New York, baseball, college. You get two guys together with just a couple of those things and they'll find a common conversation. After that, we got together occasionally in the city, and we've become great friends.

Following is my conversation with a pitcher's pitcher, who should be voted into the Hall of Fame when his time comes.

What do you think young pitchers should do to get better?

For Little League, up to 12 years old, I'd recommend long toss to build up arm strength. By long toss, I mean, 9-year-olds, 10-year-olds, maybe 90 to 100 feet. As you get older, you increase 20 to 50 feet. At 16, 17, try it at 150 to 200 feet. It stretches the arm out pretty good, as well as building arm strength. Do it for 15 to 25 throws. You don't need to do much, maybe every other day.

Obviously with Little League, at a young age, 12 to 13 years old, the best thing to do is stay away from curveballs. The ligaments and tendons still aren't developed.

What else does a coach need to do to protect the health of young arms?

A big thing when you get 14, 15 years old is a pitch limit. Some coaches have the kids go 120, 130 pitches. I like to usually go 75 pitches and get them out, have two guys split a game.

The best pitch for younger guys is the fastball, and a changeup. A changeup doesn't put any more stress on the arm, no torque or twist, like a curveball or slider does.

How did you stay in the majors for so long? What else besides your natural ability got you there?

Obviously, it's important to stay in shape, work out. My competitiveness was a big part. And the determination to learn something new every day. You're never too old to learn something new.

Even at 35 years old, when you're a veteran?

Absolutely. The game is changing every day, every year, and you have to make adjustments. The hitters are making adjustments on you, so you have to make adjustments on the hitters.

So you were changing your approach to each individual hitter as the years went on?

Sure, early in my career, I was known to throw a lot of changeups and fastballs away. Later in my career, I was throwing fastballs in, changeups in, changeups to lefties, which I never did early in my career.

Was this because you got better at some pitches, lost something on others?

Well, you try to outguess them. It's a guessing game. They try to guess what you're going to throw, and you're trying to guess what they're looking for.

You were always known for having the fire in the belly?

Fire, competitiveness, never wanting to give in, fighting until the last out. That's what I teach my kid. And respect the game. When you get on the field, run out, run off. No throwing equipment. Respect the game. It's a great game.

What was your specialty, your out pitch?

Circle change. That was the pitch that got me to the big leagues. I think it's the best pitch in baseball. I think every coach, high school coach or sandlot coach, who has any kind of knowledge, needs to learn how to throw it the correct way and teach their kids. It's a real good pitch for the kids to learn.

You put your finger like you're making the sign "OK." That's how you put your fingers on the ball, with your thumb underneath it, so it's almost like a circle, a circle OK. I like to throw it with the seams, some guys throw it across the seams. It's got different movement, different speeds. And you don't have to turn your arm over, hard, like a slider. Just throw it like a fastball. The grip will take care of the speed, and the rotation of the ball, if it's thrown correctly, will take care of the movement.

How did you know you had a guy, had him fooled?

The way he went after the pitch. Either they were way ahead of it, or they were looking for something else, swinging real hard. A lot of times I bounced it, let it fall on home plate, or bounce it right on home plate. A lot of time, it would be out of the hitter's zone by the time he was ready to hit, or ready to drop out of the zone.

You'd keep throwing it until the hitter made an adjustment. When he'd move up in the box, I'd sneak a fastball by him.

I would throw six in a row if it would get him out.

As a reliever, my philosophy was that if I could throw three pitches and get three line-drive outs, that's fine with me, too.

What do you want to be remembered for?

Number one, longevity. All-time left-handed saves leader. I was most proud of being a competitor, giving it all when I was out there.

Do you favor any particular treatments, drills?

I tell my kids that some dumbbell exercises are good. We do a lot of tubing work, Jobe exercises [named after Dr. Frank Jobe, the pioneering orthopedic surgeon behind Tommy John surgery and sports medicine], condition in the arm and the elbow. The Jobe tubing exercises are all preventive stuff, for the labrum and the rotator cuff, things like that. I tell the kids, "Don't skip the exercises, because the arm tends to break down and these exercises help you maintain strength in its parts."

After pitching I recommend icing your arm as much as you can. If it's a little sore tomorrow, then more ice.

If the elbow is sore, do a little ice massage. Pour water into a paper or Styrofoam cup, then when it freezes tear the top of the cup away and massage the sore area for about 20 minutes.

7
Fundamentals of Hitting

You can approach hitting a baseball from a number of angles, but when the bat is swung the same fundamental skills determine whether it will be a hit, a fly ball, or a whiff. Hitting doesn't have to be hard. Sometimes people dissect it like a golf swing, but I think that's looking at it wrong.

Adjustments

It's pretty basic: you see the ball, you hit it. But sometimes a player has to get to that position where he can see it to hit it. For instance, maybe the player is dropping his hands, his swing is looping. Well, have him put the bat on his shoulder for a little bit. Now it's hard for him to drop his hands. That's an adjustment.

My philosophy on teaching hitting is based on adjustments. You don't want to make it too tough. Everybody is going to hit a little differently anyway; players tend to hit instinctively. Unless a player is really struggling with a bad form we don't make any big overhauls in our camps. We adjust where the players might be off.

The Stance and Swing

Look at the major leagues. Everybody has a different stance at the plate. Sammy Sosa stood up there differently from Ken Griffey Jr., whose stance is different from what Barry Bonds once used to scare opposing pitchers. Jose Reyes is wide open at the plate. Alex Rodriguez has a classic stance, pretty straight up and down and toward the pitcher.

You could put together a pretty good coffee-table book just of Hall of Fame hitters' stances. There's Stan the Man Musial, with his arms close to his chest but left elbow high. The Great Yaz, Carl Yastrzemski, used to keep both arms extended high above his shoulders, only to drop them into the loaded position to swing. Thousands of young ballplayers were imitating him in 1967, when he won the American League Triple Crown with the most home runs (44), the most runs driven in (121), and the highest batting average (.326). Maybe the all-time champ at open stances was a guy who played for some great Detroit Tigers teams back in the '60s, second baseman Dick McAuliffe.

Common to all successful hitters, though, is that these guys, no matter where they start, arrive in the loaded position as the ball is coming to the plate. A player has to be in that loaded position in order to be successful.

Loaded Position

Regardless of where the hands start, they should have the bat back and ready at the time the batter gets into his 60/40 weight transfer (60 percent on the back side, 40 percent on the front). Dropping the weight back as the player cocks the bat should be a fairly natural movement. Otherwise, he's just swinging his arms.

The loaded position

If a hitter has too much weight forward, it's called everything from "lunging" to "swaying," but no matter what it's called, the hitter has no power and can't drive the ball. Even a singles hitter has to drive the ball.

Do not lunge in your swing.

Small Stride

When a player is hitting, he should have a small stride and keep it in his head to stay back. The player should try very hard not to be too much on his front side. You'll see a lot kids lunge, even when they take a pitch. That's no good. Hitters should be under control and balanced at all times.

Hitters should take a little step forward when they stride into the ball, but they should keep their hands back all the time. Let's say a hitter gets fooled on a pitch, say, he's looking for a fastball, but the pitcher crosses him up with something off-speed. If the hitter's hands are back, he can just go with it and hit it where it's pitched.

A hitter at any level can be fooled by a pitch, but it's more likely that a high school ballplayer will recognize what just happened. Little guys get fooled all the time because the pitching is likely more inconsistent.

If you look back at the old days, maybe at World Series games on ESPN Classic or something, you'll see some guys swing with big, exaggerated strides. Roberto Clemente would cock his body like a pistol, tugging his left knee back before his stride forward. Willie Mays was the same way; he took a big stride into the ball. But those guys were great. They were exceptions to the rule. Today, if you look around, some of the best hitters have no stride at all. Albert Pujols barely picks his foot up. Manny Ramirez really doesn't go anywhere with that front foot, either; he just picks it up. But their weight transfer is usually perfect. Of course, they're probably exceptions to the rule as well.

Young players should use a small stride so that they're always in control and balanced. It's that "athletic position" I always emphasize—balanced, in control. Remind them to keep their weight back and their hands back as long as possible.

Head Down

Keeping the head down on the ball is very important as well. Then players swing down and through (whether they're hitting off the tee or against live pitching). If players need help remembering, tell them to keep their chin down on their shoulder.

Having players keep their chin on their shoulder reminds them to maintain the proper head-down form.

The hitters' eyes have to be on the ball. They should not look at the pitcher or anything else. They want to pick up the ball as soon as they can, so they can hit it. They don't want to hit the pitcher. They don't care about him. They want to hit the ball. I know that sounds ridiculously simple, but you'd be surprised how many kids get distracted.

One of the biggest mistakes young kids make is pulling their heads out as they swing. Their arms and shoulders move their heads so that they're looking down the line afterward. Tell them, "You don't want to look like one of those bobblehead dolls at the plate. You can save that for when you make the major leagues and are given a special night with a promotional giveaway to the first 14,000 fans."

Follow Through

The follow-through is just as important as the rest, and I have a good way to see if a player is doing it. I mentioned it earlier because we talk about it in our camp. I call it the "wrinkle effect." A guy who is hitting the ball properly with the right power should have wrinkles on the back leg of his pants—the right side for a right-handed hitter or the left side for a left-handed hitter.

Have someone take pictures of your players as they are swinging. If they have that wrinkle in their back pants leg, their weight is where it should be.

Players must not just swing to swing—they must swing for solid contact. Every swing must have a purpose. They should make a good solid swing. Today's major leaguers say it so often after hitting a game-winning home run that it's becoming a new baseball cliché, but it's true: "I just wanted to put a good swing on it."

So, to review. Hitting is very basic and rooted in solid fundamentals. The player should be in the loaded position and balanced when the ball is pitched. He should stay back with his hands back and away from his body and keep his head down. Then he should take a small stride, with the weight transfer from back to front. He should follow through the swing, level, with his eyes still on the ball.

Players should practice these fundamentals with drills that will improve and coordinate their muscle memory. Remember that ath-

Notice the back pant leg—this is what we call the "wrinkle effect."

letic skills greatly increase when players learn the proper way early and reinforce it with repetition.

Drills and Developmental Tools

I work the following exercises and tools into my practices, whether it's at a camp for kids or with my college players.

The Batting Tee

The most inexpensive tool you can buy is a batting tee. For $20 and a couple of baseballs, your players can build muscle memory hitting the ball against a screen or against a wall. Yankee great and hitting guru Don Mattingly took 100 to 150 swings every day off a tee, and he had a .307 lifetime batting average. Albert Pujols also religiously hits off a tee in the clubhouse every day, and he's putting up numbers similar to the early likes of Joe DiMaggio and Ted Williams. Bobby Bonds, one-time hitting coach for the Indians, father of Barry, and outfield mate of Willie Mays, was also a big tee proponent.

Just get one of those rubber tees that usually stand on a home plate–shaped piece of hard rubber. If your players want to get one to practice on their own, they can take it to a park where there is a

The batter's weight transfers from his back leg (left) to his front leg (right) as he hits off the tee.

backstop, put the tee up a few feet from the backstop, and hit balls into the fence. It's as simple as that. They can do it in their yard with a hockey or lacrosse net. Your players can do it all by themselves, and you can do it as a station for your team. The repetition of hitting over and over coaxes the players' bodies into reacting more automatically.

Building Muscle Memory

When athletes play sports, any sport, they exercise some muscles that are different from the ones they normally use to walk, stand, talk, and go to school. The big muscles get more of a workout than they may be used to, sure, but there are also smaller muscles that

A head-down, level swing off the tee

come more into play. Of course, the more players work these muscles out, the stronger they get. It becomes easier for them to do the motions required, such as swinging a bat, executing a throw, or getting a good jump on the base path.

When players are using the tee, they should focus on balance. Their weight transfer from back to front should be smooth and balanced, and they should swing through the ball, all the things we talked about previously.

Have the players put their chin on their shoulder and practice "chin-to-shoulder," "chin-to-shoulder" strokes with the bat. They should swing down and through the ball, watching it all the way.

A good practice is for the players to aim to hit the ball to the right center field part of the fence (if they are right-handed; lefties should hit to left center field). In other words, they should not pull it. Yanking the ball to left field pulls the player's head up, and they'll be grounding out more often than anything else if they hit it, because the bat comes off the ball, driving it down. They're also no longer keeping their eye on the ball if their head isn't still. That brings a lot of strikeouts.

With this exercise, your players are learning the feeling of what the body goes through to connect to right center. It's a feeling you want them to be familiar with.

Super Stick

I have something I call a super stick. We use it to warm up with in the on-deck circle. You might have seen them in major league games; they're becoming more common. My father first made one for me when I was a youngster. A super stick is a 35-inch steel rod that we tape up, and it's eight pounds evenly distributed through the whole thing.

I tell my guys to take 100 swings with the super stick a day, in sets of 25 reps. If a player takes 100 swings a day with that thing, when he gets up to the plate, the bat feels like a feather. Players can swing it 25 reps at a time in the on-deck circle, or at every practice. It will strengthen their hands and their forearms.

We also have one for the younger kids that's only about three pounds. It's a shorter, thinner version, as you might expect, and it's only about 32 to 33 inches long. The younger kids should swing it a lot, though it depends on their size. I did it when I was younger and it really helped me.

When your players swing with the super stick, they should not be swinging fast. They need to take nice, level, even strokes with good technique. Have them stop in the middle of a swing and pivot back and forth, and they will improve their hand strength.

Soft Toss

You've probably seen it in commercials if you watch much sports television. In soft toss, a hitter stands facing the screen, and a guy off to his side, either an adult or another player, softly lobs baseballs continuously in front of the hitter. The hitter gets the ball consistently in the hitting zone and smacks it into the screen. If you have an L-shaped screen normally used for pitching batting practice, the player doing the soft tosses can be in front of the hitter. So much the better.

When you soft toss, make the ball come to the same part of the plate every time. The hitter should concentrate on keeping his head down and hitting it up the middle. This is, again, repetition work that will build muscle memory.

A variation on soft toss is to use Nerf-style foam balls. We also like to use a Jugs Lite-Flight Machine. It throws the same Nerf-style balls.

Soft toss with a coach

Machine Consistency

If you can, have your players practice against a pitching machine for consistent pitches. Batting practice is faster and a hitter gets the ball more reliably in the same place and for strikes when you have a machine. These things aren't the big giants they used to be, and not nearly as expensive. They're readily available in stores, by catalog, or through the Internet.

These machines, as I have mentioned earlier, have a lot of other uses, too. You can use them for fielding practice for pop-ups or fly balls. We seem to have ours in use all the time at some part of the field.

Keep in mind that repetition is the key. Kids aren't going to learn it all in a half hour or a day, so use these drills regularly.

Bunting

If a player can't bunt, he can't play for me. It's as simple as that. There's nothing in the fundamental game more basic than bunting. In this modern, bang-bang, home run–crazy era, that seems to get lost on a lot of guys. Some games are won by walk-off home runs, but I'll bet that many more games are won by solid baseball fundamentals.

The bunt can do so many things. Players can bunt to get a runner into scoring position. They can bunt for base hits. They can draw an infield in just by the threat of bunting. They can draw the infield in by a reputation for bunt base hits. If a player draws the infield in and swings away, his batting average goes up 50 points.

Before batting practice, we always have a round of bunts: everyone has to lay down two sacrifice bunts and two bunts for base hits. (Bunting for base hits raised my college average from .350–.370 to .420.) Players have to know how to bunt.

When we separate into groups so that everybody gets a workout at the same time (remember, always keep the kids busy), we sometimes have an area where we'll teach fake bunts for hits. This is for the more advanced kids, but it's a good station.

How to Bunt

Teach your players to bunt using the following steps:

- Bring the bat around when the pitcher is in his windup, not before he starts.
- Square around to face the pitcher with the bat balanced in your hands. Don't just drop the bat low without squaring around.
- Keep your eyes where the bat head is.
- Drop down to an athletic position, with the head of the bat on a 45-degree angle and your eyes at the barrel.

The bunter squares around.

His eyes are focused on the bat head.

The bunter (left) and his instructor (right) stand ready, with the bat at a 45-degree angle.

The pitch is on a trajectory to go low for a ball—as with a pitch above the eyes, the correct response is to pull the bat back.

- If the pitch is above your eyes, pull the bat back. It's a ball.
- If the ball is below your eyes (remember, you're square and in an athletic position), extend your hands out in front of the plate and catch the ball with the bat.
- To control the direction of the bunt, shift the barrel of the bat to either the left or right side.

FOR A SACRIFICE. With a man on first, get the bunt down either line. With runners at first and second base, bunt up the third-base line to make the third baseman come in to field the ball. It has to be far enough to make him come in, though, because if the pitcher or catcher fields it, he's got a clear shot at third.

FOR A BASE HIT. Use either a drag bunt or a push bunt. A right-hander would drag it down to third base or push it between the pitcher and the first baseman. A left-hander has an advantage because he starts a few steps ahead of a right-handed hitter on the way to first. A left-handed hitter would drag it down toward first.

A drag bunt down the third-base side for a potential base hit

When players are bunting for base hits, they should put it on the line and bunt it "fair or foul." When righties drag it down the third-base line, if the ball stays fair they should get the hit, because it's always a tough play for a third baseman. If the ball rolls foul, they get another chance, provided, of course, there are less than two strikes. If they bunt it too far to the pitcher, they're going to be out, so teach them to bunt down the lines.

Teaching Kids Not to Fear the Ball

The biggest problem for a lot of kids when they're just learning the game is that they're afraid of the ball. They're right, it can hurt. But so can a lot of the crazy things they do, things that almost stop our hearts so much we're glad we miss some of them. So, like a lot of life, it may take some getting used to.

My dad taught me never to be afraid of the baseball, whether I was hitting or catching it. Every now and then, when I took batting practice, he would intentionally hit me with a pitch. He didn't try to hurt me, but he would explain that when the ball does hit you, though you may feel pain for a minute, by the time the next pitch is thrown you will have forgotten about it.

The old saw, "Shake it off," really kind of works. "Put some dirt on it" is ridiculous, but you rub it a little, laugh at yourself, and on you go. Tomorrow you may have a bruise, but what game we play doesn't bring a few bruises?

It's the same for learning the fundamentals of catching a baseball. Most kids today, as well as parents, don't take the time to play catch. So there are too many kids who are afraid of the baseball. They'll stand to the side of the ball and almost contort themselves to catch it. I feel that players must spend as much time catching and throwing as they do hitting. Maybe more, because it's easier to do. They can just grab a glove and a ball with anybody available to play catch with.

Players must work on these fundamentals consistently to get to the next level of baseball and continue growing in the game.

I'll have parents with a kid who is five or six years old, and they want to put him in my camp. We use some discretion with the little ones, because in addition to the baseball part and the level of development is the issue of endurance. It's not easy being out there for six hours when you're six years old.

The other big factor, though, is this: The first thing they say to me is, "You ought to see my son hit the ball." So I ask them, "Yeah, but can he catch it?" Because what can happen is that when somebody hits the ball, or somebody throws it to him, and he gets hit in the face, or gets hurt, he may never want to play baseball again. It could leave an indelible mark, physically and psychologically. Players should take as much time learning to catch the ball as hitting the ball. That's very, very important.

8

Fundamentals of Baserunning

Good teams can run the bases. That may sound funny. You might say, "What's so hard about that? First you run to first, then you run to second." Well, there's more to it than that, not a lot more, but running bases in a fundamentally sound, aggressive way wins ball games. You can steal runs, you can manufacture runs, you can put pressure on the opponent's defense and create errors. Remember, at its core baseball is a simple game: if you have one more run than the other guy at the end of the game, you win.

You can also run into outs, prematurely end an inning, and ruin scoring chances. That's going to happen from time to time if you're aggressive. So you pick your spots to be aggressive, don't take unnecessary chances, and run the bases in a fundamentally smart way. Sure, it'll backfire occasionally, but if you're doing it right, you should come out way ahead.

You can also run into inning-killing outs by not running smart, not playing heads-up. That can happen due to mental errors, or maybe the kids just don't know what to do in a situation. That's why we want to teach our kids how running the bases is more than just being fast. Playing smart, athletic baseball is the key to advancing to the next level.

Running to First

You'd be surprised, but a lot kids will stop at first base instead of running through the bag. Have them practice swinging the bat and just running down the line, running as hard as they can. Tell them, "When you stop, you've got less time. You're slowing yourself down in your race to be safe. But if you go through the base, it even fools the umpire sometimes."

Everyone lines up and practices running through first base without stopping.

Remind everybody to turn toward foul territory after they pass first. If players make no attempt to advance, they're not going to be called out if they turn the wrong way and walk back to the bag, but it's best to do it the right way—as always. They do need to be ready to take off for second if the ball is thrown past the first baseman, though. Tell your guys to keep their heads up, and be sure to have somebody coaching at first to help them out. A coach is very important here because the player should be focused on getting to first; he needs another set of eyes to keep track of who is backing up the play and where the ball is. Of course, if the ball goes out of play, the runner is awarded second base.

Another thing that kids may pick up from big leaguers is the nonchalant run to first base when they figure they're going to be out. Tell them that's not a model to imitate. You can never anticipate a routine play to be routine, especially in youth baseball. There's always chance for error, for the wind to blow, for somebody to stumble. Your players have got to run hard each and every time they hit the ball, on foul balls too, especially on dribblers down the line that could turn fair.

Usually, by the time kids are 11 or 12, leagues start using the third-strike rule, where the catcher has to catch the pitched ball in the air, before it hits the ground. Players have to be schooled to take off hard when they swing and miss with a ball in the dirt, a dropped ball, or one that gets away from the catcher. Sometimes kids will be so busy feeling sorry for themselves because they struck out that they forget about it. Stay on them to be alert; the play may not be over. Every time you force the other team to make an extra throw, there's a chance for an error.

Rounding Bases

When players get a base hit, they don't want to run through the first-base bag. Your first-base coach should indicate to the player whether he should round it and stay, or round it and dig hard for second. Coaches need to make these calls, too, on stretching for a double or triple. The windmilling arm and shouts of "Go, go, go!" should do the trick. Or the stop sign, the hands extended in a pretty universal gesture, not peculiar to baseball coaches.

To cut first base on a short hit, the player should veer outside the baseline and hit the inside corner of the base with whatever foot he's getting there with. If he's staying, he should round the bag and look up, then get back. If he's digging for second, he should dig. He shouldn't go halfway. Once a player is committed, he's got to go as hard as he can. It's called no-man's-land for a reason: you don't want to be there.

For running through second and third, a player again wants to cut the bag on the inside, though the veer may be a little less pronounced.

Sliding

At our camps, we practice sliding every day, first thing. We even have a sliding contest at the end of the week. That's the importance I place in learning the proper slide.

We tell the kids to run really hard and get a leg underneath. They have to slide on their backsides. "Get your hands up and slide on your butt." A lot of kids slide with their hands down, but they can hurt their wrists doing this, so you have to be very careful.

Kids in camp always ask me about headfirst slides. My answer is no. It's dangerous. You can get your hands stepped on. You can sprain or break your wrist or fingers. You don't get there any faster, maybe slower, because you have to change your momentum a little bit to launch yourself forward. Sliding on your backside, you use your momentum. And when the second baseman slaps that tag on

Cutting first base short by veering outside and then hitting the inside corner

The proper way to slide after running hard—feet first with one leg underneath. If the player were sliding into second base, he'd be in a perfect position to pop up with his leg underneath.

you, your leg is much bigger and able to take the blow. If you get a little bruise, it'll heal quickly.

Players can also sprain an ankle pretty easily if they do a half-slide. I've seen it a lot. Kids start to slide too late or change their minds in the middle. They can't do that. They have to commit to the slide and go down. If they practice until they're perfect, it becomes second nature. If it's a new season and your players know how to slide perfectly, that doesn't mean you shouldn't reinforce it with a little practice. There's sometimes a little part of the mind that resists throwing oneself on the ground, and he who hesitates is lost.

Pop-Up Slides

Another big advantage to sliding feet first with the leg tucked under is that the player can execute a pop-up slide easily. You've seen the major league players do this often. Jose Reyes swipes second and the catcher throws high and into center field. Watch Reyes stand right back up on his feet and take third. Even sliding headfirst he still manages to use that leg underneath and the momentum he has propelling him toward the bag to push his weight up and into a standing position again.

Pop-up slides are a product of momentum. If a player is running hard and he slides, he'll come up automatically. If he doesn't run fast enough, he's not going to pop up. If he runs hard and does it right, when he hits the bag he is not only going to keep himself from going past the base and getting tagged out, he's also ready to go to the next base if there's an error or misplay.

Hook Slides

Sometimes, though, a player will want to do a hook slide to avoid a tag. For instance, he's coming into second and he sees that the shortstop has to reach back to the left field side to take the throw. The runner wants to make as small a target as he can for the tag, and he wants to make the opponent reach as far as possible. In this case he would begin to slide slightly to the right of the bag. When his extended front leg reaches the bag, he should relax it and keep it on the base as he comes around with his body. His foot stays "hooked" on the front side of the bag. He must remember to call "time" before dusting himself off.

Another time a player should slide a little to the side of the base is when he is coming home and the catcher has the plate partially blocked. This is another instance where the player wants to slide away from the catcher or the throw. Throws to the catcher are more likely to be off-line if they are coming from the outfield. In fact, they're generally more likely to be off because players will clutch a little trying to get a guy at the plate.

The runner uses a hook-slide approach, sliding away from the catcher, to avoid the tag.

If the catcher has a little devil in him (or he's just a smart ball-player), he may try to fool the runner by standing there passively as if the ball weren't coming; the runner can't see where the throw is coming from. The runner shouldn't be looking; he's got nowhere else to go now. He should look to his teammate who is the on-deck hitter. The on-deck player should be there where the runner can see him indicating with his hands whether to slide or cross the plate standing up.

Leads and Stealing

Here's a basic rule of thumb on leads. When a player is on first base, he should take two pretty good steps off the base. One, two, cross-over. That's a pretty good lead. I like my kids to dive back all the time—that way they know they've got a maximum lead. If a player doesn't have to dive back on a throw to the base, he's not off far enough and needs to take a bigger lead next time.

As a player gets a little bit older, let's say he takes that lead. When the pitcher is on the rubber and he's got his sign and takes his stretch position, that is the time to take a little extra lead. The pitcher is looking home, chances are he won't notice the runner taking a little extra nudge before he looks back his way. The runner looks like he

"One, two, crossover" for a good lead

hasn't moved, but he's got an extra foot or so. That can make all the difference when a runner is stealing a base.

Now, a player is on first and you give him the steal sign. When does he break for second? As an indicator, the runner can use either the pitcher's front foot or his back foot on the rubber. If the back foot comes off the rubber, the runner has to get back to first. If it stays on the rubber, he has to go.

However, if the runner wants to get a good break, he has to watch that front foot. Once that foot comes off the ground and is pointed straight toward home, rather than with the toe pointed to the runner, the runner can go. If the toe points toward him, he has to get back to first; if it goes home, he should break for second.

Tagging Up on Fly Balls

When you've got a runner on second or third base and a fly ball is hit into the outfield with less than two outs, you want to see if you can take advantage of the situation and either score the run from third or get the runner from second over to third, where he can score on more plays (a runner can score from third on an error, a sharply hit single to the outfield, an infield single, a wild pitch, a passed ball, a balk, a sacrifice fly, even a foul pop caught tumbling into the seats). If you have guys on both bases and the ball is hit to deep right or center field, you might be able to move them both up. Generally, it's pretty tough to tag up and go to third from second on a ball hit to left. The relative strength of the outfielders' arms also has to be considered.

The runner can leave the base when the ball touches the leather of the outfielder's glove. He doesn't have to wait until it's caught. If the fly ball first bounces off one guy's glove, but is caught by another, the runner can still leave when it hits that first glove.

When a player is running the bases and a ball is hit to the outfield, if he doesn't know if it will drop or not, he should be about halfway to the next base.

At first base, the runner can retreat to the base if the fielder catches it.

Getting ready to steal second, the runner sees the pitcher's toe pointing toward home, takes off, and runs hard.

At second base, the likelihood of the fly being caught determines where the runner should be. He wants to be halfway if it looks like it'll take a circus catch, so he can sprint home if the ball isn't caught. In the event it is caught, the runner can give up advancing to third, fly back to the bag, and see if the contortions the fielder had to take for his Web-gem catch have made it tough for him to recover in time to throw him out.

At third base, you have to weigh how far out the ball is hit. Usually, the runner will stay closer to the bag to tag up if the fielder catches it; most of the time if he doesn't, the runner can still get home.

On a deep fly, where the runner knows he can make the bag easily, he should count a beat after the ball touches the fielder's glove so there's no doubt in the umpire's mind he didn't leave early.

Tagging Up on Foul Balls

If a foul ball is caught on the fly for an out, a runner can tag and advance. In this case he should be right on the bag, in an athletic position, ready to burst down the line. He needn't be halfway, because if it drops, he can't advance anyway. In some cases, a smart fielder may want to let a catchable foul drop to keep a decisive run from scoring (because he's unlikely to get the man at the plate, whether because of distance or an odd angle).

Rundowns

If a runner finds himself caught between two bases, he should try to stay in the rundown as long as possible. He shouldn't give up on it. The opportunities for error multiply each time somebody has to throw the ball, and if the opposing team hasn't practiced rundowns as your team has, you'll be getting some runs out of it. There are almost as many botched rundowns in youth baseball as there are batters pulling their heads out at the plate (no, I exaggerate, but there are plenty).

There are real opportunities for other runners when a teammate is caught in a rundown. Those runners should be advancing.

If the rundown is behind a runner on second or third, that runner should take advantage of the fielders' distraction and move up.

The fielders should be alert enough to make a play on him, but usually, if he's smart about it, they won't be quick enough and both runners will be safe. This is one of the things I'm talking about when I say "aggressive" baserunning.

If the rundown is in front of a runner, he should still move up. You can't have two runners on the same bag, but at least you'll have the advance bag, because the chances are the guy in the rundown is going to be out anyway. For instance, Bobby is caught in a rundown between third and home, but Mikey is on second base. With less than two outs, Mikey should run to third despite the fact that it could be a safe base for Bobby. Now, when Bobby is out, even if he retreats to the bag, escaping the tag, at least you have a runner at third.

Taking the Extra Base on Infield Plays

When a runner is on second and the ball is hit on the infield, when does he advance to third? First of all, after the ball was pitched he should have taken a good secondary lead, so he's on the base path pretty much in front of the shortstop. If the ball is hit behind him, in other words, to his left, he should go to third. If the shortstop is going to his left to field the ball, he'll have a tough time turning his body in order to throw the runner out at third (and let's hope he tries). If it's hit to second or first, the hitter has done his job of moving the runner to third, especially if he gets there with one out.

If it's hit in front of the runner, either to the third baseman or the shortstop moving to his right, the runner should stop. He shouldn't necessarily retreat to second, because he may be able to go to third when they make their throw to first. But the shortstop moving to the hole will be able to glove the ball backhand and make a throw in the direction he is going. It might be bang-bang, but he's likely to be out.

Sometimes, with a runner on third, you may want to tell the runner to go home "on contact." That means when the ball is hit on the ground in the infield, the runner would make his burst for home. On third, the runner should take a walking lead as the pitcher delivers and when it's hit, go, without hesitation. In other situations, you may want to be more cautious and see where the ball is hit before sending the runner.

Drills

Just like everything else, we have baserunning drills. Often you can incorporate them with fielding drills and situation drills. I'll give you a few examples.

Rundowns

We practice rundowns consistently. As I said previously, there are plenty of opportunities for error, and practicing rundowns improves both our fielding and baserunning skills. This is not something, either, that the kids need do only at practice. It's great fun whenever a bunch of children get together, at a picnic, at the park, a family barbecue, wherever, because they can involve all the little kids, too. We used to call it "Pickle," and we'd play it all the time.

Timing on the Bases

We time the kids when they sprint from home to first, and from first to third base. Then we have contests to see who has the best time. Sometimes kids can improve dramatically.

Situations

I feel that one of the most important skills for a ballplayer is knowing where to throw the ball, where to be on the field in any given situation, and what he's doing on the bases when the ball is hit somewhere. Every player must be thinking, "What do I do next, given A, B, C, etc.?" Baserunning situations can combine with fielding situation drills. Don't neglect one for the other. Make sure the kids are paying attention to their role in the drill and listening to what the other guys are hearing so that when it becomes their turn, they'll know what to do.

A Catcher's Take on Pitching

Following are some tips for pitchers based on my years as a catcher.

Throw Strikes

You'll get the edge from umpires if they're used to you throwing strikes. Even in Little League. If you're a little bit wild, you'll lose the umpire—and you'll lose your players behind you because if somebody suddenly hits the ball, they're not going to be ready.

Johan Santana is going to get more calls than a rookie pitcher, because the umpires know Johan Santana throws strikes, and he's around the plate. Rookie pitchers have it tougher. For instance, if you're watching the Yankees games, Ian Kennedy and Phil Hughes don't get the same calls as Andy Pettitte or Mike Mussina, because they're more established guys and they're around the plate a little bit more.

Throw Inside

Even Hall of Fame greats Willie Mays and "Hammering Hank" Aaron did not hit Bob Gibson very well. Mays hit just .196 against Gibby, and Aaron was little better at .215. Mays told Bob Costas on an HBO special that when he met Gibson off the field, when a friend brought the Cardinals' pitcher to his house, Mays was surprised to see Gibson wearing glasses.

" 'Why are you wearing those,' I asked. He said, 'Because I need them.' After that I was never easy in the box against him," Mays said. Gibson was known to throw inside, dust hitters, and even bean hitters if he thought it necessary to maintain order. You didn't admire a home run or trot slowly around the bases on

Gibby. He threw very hard. "I never hit as many guys as they say I did," he complained on the same show.

Most good hitters like to reach out over the plate, get their arms extended. So pitchers need to stake some claim to the inner half of the plate. Pitching inside does that.

9
Fielding

Defense is a big key to winning baseball games. Ask any manager what he needs to do to win and he will tell you, "We need to make routine plays and catch the ball." You can control the game with defense. You always feel that you are in the game and playing well when you play good defense; it's what keeps you in the game until your offense comes alive.

Whitey Herzog, former manager of the St. Louis Cardinals, used to say that shortstop Ozzie Smith saved 20 games a year with his skill in the field. That's a lot of games when you consider how many pennants have come down to the last day of the season and one game in the standings. Yankees shortstop Derek Jeter will forever be remembered for the play in the 2001 American League playoffs against the Oakland A's when he came out of nowhere to take an errant throw and flip it to catcher Jorge Posada for the out at the plate. And let's not forget the unbelievable play of Yankees third baseman Graig Nettles against the Los Angeles Dodgers in the 1978 World Series. All of these players made themselves great defensive players. That is the beauty of defense—you can take hundreds and hundreds of ground balls and get to the Hall of Fame.

Regarding the play that Jeter made: it's not often you can say it, but that fielding play won the game and probably turned the series around for the Yankees. Willie Randolph, a coach for the Yanks at the time, says that the team worked Derek in practice as a "floater" cutoff man in that situation. Because Jeter has great baseball instincts, he was the right man for that play in the right spot. Instincts cannot be completely taught because they are in the player. But those instincts lie dormant until the player does all the hard work, listening to coaches through the years and watching baseball as a kid. It's then that it clicks in the player's mind, and then he can react. If a player reacts and succeeds, he becomes great like Derek Jeter.

Ozzie Smith was called "the Wizard" because of his acrobatic plays. That's another kind of instinctive playing. Ozzie was magical at times, but he once said, "I stay ready and on my toes at all times. I know where to play hitters, watch where they are being pitched, and most of all I anticipate where the ball will be hit."

Extra Outs Are Killers

Just as walks are self-destructive to pitchers, errors behind the pitcher will destroy both his and the team's self-confidence. Anytime you give the other team an extra out, your pitcher has to throw that many more strikes, that many more pitches, and the other team has another chance for at least one more run than it should have. It's not just the errors themselves, you put good fielding behind your pitcher and he will improve simply because he won't feel like he has to strike everybody out.

This is a big reason why managers and coaches sacrifice some offense for someone who can make the routine plays. This is why we stress defense at our camps. I feel that too many youth league coaches spend too much time with hitting and not enough time with field-ing practice. In our camps, we stress ground balls two times each week. We hit them right at the fielders, then to their right, and then to their left. We make them field ground balls bare-handed, make force outs, and make the right decisions on bunt plays.

But an error is to be instantly forgotten, at least until after the frame is over and a coach can review what may have gone wrong. It could have been nothing more than a brain freeze: a last-minute doubt in the player's mind that he could make the play. This is not the time or the place to doubt that player's ability or commitment. That player needs another chance and that chance immediately, the less said the better. If he freezes again, then he must do the play at practice until it becomes automatic, so that in a game, muscle memory takes over.

If, on the other hand, the player has a problem with technique, go over the problem on the bench, make sure he understands. Call over some of the other guys who may be having the same problem from time to time. They may not want to hear it all again, but a good team begins to understand that the price of winning is consistency, and if you have to listen to the old man reinforce a lesson, down the road, you'll thank him for it. Every coach I've ever had who has pushed me further than I really wanted to be pushed at the time turned out to be right later on.

Back to the field.

Throwing the Ball Around

Players can't let one error or bad play get to them. It's nothing more than a bad tee shot. They must forget about it, immediately. They must not boot the ball and recover, only to pick it up and throw it away. They don't want to compound their mistakes. They need to control their emotions. If they can realistically still get the out, they must go for it.

One of the most common problems with young teams is throw-ing the ball around, making one error after another on a play, trying to make up for the first error or getting a little frantic as a base run-ner advances. That's why practicing situations is fundamental.

Getting Loose

When players first get out on the field, or before they go into any game, they need to loosen up and stretch those muscles they've been sitting on. It's important for them to run a few quick laps, or jog in place, to get the blood flowing in their legs before they do any stretching exercises. You don't want to stretch cold, brittle muscles and tendons.

For throwing, they should loosen up their arms by throwing easy at first, their fingers across the seams, using their legs as leverage when they throw. They should always step in the direction they are going to throw.

Proper Fielding Position

Let's get into the proper way to field ground balls. Before every pitch the players should get themselves in a ready, athletic position—on the balls of their feet, glove down, alert, maybe chattering a little bit, encouraging the pitcher. This way they're in a ready position before the ball is pitched. Let's say the ball is hit to a player. He should approach the ball, staying down, and as the ball approaches, slow down and get his hands out in front of him—both hands out in front of him.

Players should catch the ball with two hands. We call it the "alligator hand position," where a player catches the ball like an alligator

Preparing to field the ball with both hands out in front

opening its mouth. That's how we like players to field a ground ball. The player fields the ball with his glove open below and his bare hand on top, brings it in to himself, takes his crow hop, points his shoulder, and throws it over to first base. It's pretty simple.

We emphasize this with the "flat glove drill." It is like using a ping-pong paddle to catch a ground ball. It forces the players to use two hands.

Fielding Fundamentals

I emphasize "two hands" every chance I get. Don't be seduced by what I call the "TV effect." You get this from watching too many

The player fields the ball, transfers, and gets in position to make the throw.

game highlights on television, the great plays that make everybody gasp. For every ball that David Wright grabs one-handed and throws to first, he fields 30 with both hands. You can't make the great plays until the routine stuff is routine for you. And don't try to make it look harder than it is. If you can get two hands on it, you're more likely to make the out. Outs are what count, and routine outs count just the same as the spectacular outs.

This is an important idea for players to keep in their head when they're fielding ground balls: if they keep their hands inside their legs, most of the time their momentum is carrying them forward toward where they want to throw. Think of that. If they're always getting two hands on the ball, they're probably doing it, but that's what they should see when they visualize how they want to approach a ground ball. It helps for them to see what they want to do in their head before they do it; it's the athletic approach.

I said this earlier, but it bears repeating. Players should grip the ball with four seams so that the throw will have more spin and will carry with greater authority to the player receiving the throw. If they grip the ball with two seams, it will sink and move, and that almost always will result in a bad throw. And if they throw the ball flat-footed instead of taking a crow hop, the ball will dive and have no power behind it.

Charging the ball, the fielder keeps his hands in front of his legs so he can see the ball.

Have your players practice taking ground balls and automatically feeling for the right way to throw the ball. It is much easier than it sounds, but practice makes it more perfect.

If a player has to reach backhand to catch the ball, he should plant his back foot, make his crow hop, and throw. If he doesn't have time for the crow hop, he should use the momentum generated from stopping his body, the little recoil, to add thrust and power.

An infielder throws differently from an outfielder or a pitcher. The baseball should be cocked at his ear, snapped, and thrown stiff on a line. Of course, there's some trajectory when it's going from the

The fielder comes up, takes a crow hop, and is ready to make a strong throw.

third baseman or shortstop to first, but an infielder makes a shorter, sharper throw.

Infielders should always remember to get their arm back and get good extension. They should point that lead shoulder to their target, plant, and use their back leg to get good power on their throws.

The Infield

First, let's go over the core responsibilities for each position, and then we'll get into a little more specifics on skills.

Second Base

The second baseman has five key responsibilities:

- Cover the ground between shortstop and first base (including over the middle), pop flies down the right field line, pops into short right, and center fields. This area increases when the first baseman is holding a runner on first base.
- Turn the double play that starts on the left side of the infield, from shortstop or third, or sometimes from the pitcher or catcher.

With the ball cocked at the fielder's ear, a strong throw will follow.

- Cover first base on bunt plays fielded by the first baseman, or on a double play initiated by the first baseman when he ranges far off the bag.
- Relay cutoff throws on hits to right field or right center; depending on the strength of his arm, he may take cutoff throws from center.
- On an attempted steal, take the throw from the catcher and tag out the runner trying to steal. Rule of thumb: beginning with high school baseball, if a right-handed hitter is up, the second baseman normally covers for the steal. The shortstop will cover for a left-handed hitter.

Shortstop

For many youth teams, the shortstop will be the best athlete on the team because it is the toughest infield spot. He must have the greatest range, be quicker, and have the best arm. He'll also probably handle the most chances. The shortstop has at least five key duties:

- Cover his position between the hole behind third base and second base (including up the middle), pop flies down the left field line, pops into short left, and center fields. If the shortstop is going for a ball hit up the middle, he can't go after it at an angle where he's going to catch the ball in the outfield. He has to go straight at the ball and dive, because if the hitter is a decent runner he's not going to get him from the outfield. The shortstop must catch the ball on the infield surface somewhere. You'll never get the runner from the outfield, unless he's a very slow runner.
- Turn the double play that starts on the left side of the infield, from shortstop or third, or sometimes from the pitcher or catcher.
- Cover third base on bunt plays fielded by the third baseman.
- Relay cutoff throws on hits to left field or left center; depending on the strength of his arm he usually will take cutoff throws from center.
- On an attempted steal, take the throw from the catcher and tag out the runner trying to steal. On some plays, with runners on

first and third, the shortstop may cut just behind the pitcher to take the throw from the catcher and try to thwart a double steal at home.

Third Base

The third baseman occupies the "hot corner," so named because even in youth league baseball a batted ball can scream out at him. The ball is sometimes hit very sharply, and it takes quick reflexes to grab the liners, short-hoppers, and hot comet ground balls. It also takes a strong arm; it's the longest throw on the infield, other than maybe a shortstop's deep pitch from the hole. The best arms on your infield will be at short and third. The third baseman has at least five key responsibilities:

- Cover his position at third base and range as far to his left as he can. The third baseman cuts off any grounders heading toward the shortstop; he is closer to first, and his momentum will be carrying him forward to make the throw. He also has to get pop flies down the left field line and any foul pops he can get to. The third baseman should always call off the pitcher if he can reach a pop-up on the infield; it's much easier for him to look up and get under the ball because he is not coming off the mound.

- Start the double play if a ground ball comes to him, firing to the second baseman when he has a play. A double play is rarely turned at third, but a hard grounder with runners at first and second can result in double play with a quick step on third base and throw to first. Third basemen should always remember this: Get the lead runner. Make a good throw. It's better to get one out instead of none out.

- Bunts. The third baseman will usually find himself covering the bunt. On expected bunts, he should play in from the bag, closer to home. With older kids, we practice one-handed catch-and-throws to first, because sometimes, with a well-placed bunt, it's the only way you'll get the out. Other times the third baseman covers the base on bunt plays fielded by the catcher, pitcher, or first baseman.

- Relay cutoff throws. The third sacker is the cutoff man when a ball is hit to left field. He should be lined up by the catcher and stand between third base and the pitcher's mound.
- On an attempted steal, take the throw from the catcher and tag out the runner trying to steal. The third baseman should reach the bag so that he can straddle it diagonally and take the throw near the sliding runner. He should not be afraid to stick it to him. But by all means, he must not let it get by into left field; that means a run.

First Base

The first baseman must be able to catch the ball. For young teams, you really need a guy with good hands. As teams get older the skill set increases, but a first bagger who can grab the ball no matter where it's thrown is a gift for any team. He will save the day many times.

One mistake I see a lot of kids make playing first base is that they commit too early. For instance, the ball is hit to third and the third baseman hasn't thrown the ball yet, and the first baseman has run to the bag and is stretching already. He's standing there stretched out, but then the throw is bad, and all of sudden, it's coming in over his head, way to the right. There's no way he can get to it now; he's already compromised himself into the stretch position.

The first baseman stretches to receive the throw.

The first baseman needs to stretch for the ball, but only when he knows where the throw is going.

When the ball is hit on the infield, the first baseman should move toward the bag and stand far enough away from it so that he can reach back with either foot and touch it. He should face whoever is going to throw the ball to him, third baseman, shortstop, or second baseman. Then, when the ball is coming and he sees the throw, he can move his feet, shuffle his feet, in case the ball is thrown errantly.

Catcher

The catcher is the field general of the baseball game. Everything is in front of him; he's the only one who sees it all. He's in every play. He should be directing the guys, reminding everybody of how many outs there are (and middle infielders should be reminding the outfielders).

When the catcher is trying to throw a guy out trying to steal second base, he should always try to gain a little bit of ground. There are two positions behind the plate. There's the regular position when there's nobody on, and there's the straddle position where the catcher is in a little less of a relaxed crouch, more a ready position to throw. When the runner is stealing, if the catcher has to catch the ball, he should gain a little bit of ground, turn his body, and make a

The catcher's regular position with no runners on (left) and straddle position (right), with runners on base

good, solid throw from his ear. He can't be too long. When a catcher is long, he's easier to steal on. He has to be quick behind the plate. It's all about quickness. He has to have a strong arm.

In high school and college everyone stresses quickness. But let's not forget that in order to throw out a runner stealing, the throw must be accurate. Base-stealing is something you can put a limit on. I tell my college guys, our pitchers should pay more attention and hold runners closer, and our catchers can be more deliberate, but they have to be more accurate. In other words, a reaction time of 1.8 seconds does not impress me if the catcher doesn't get the baseball to second base. I would rather see 2.0 seconds and an accurate throw. Of course these are college times, but the principle is the same.

When there is going to be a play at the plate, the catcher should never block the plate where someone can come in and knock him over. When he's waiting for a throw from the outfield, he should have both heels somewhere near the corners of home plate. Why? Because he wants to show the runner part of home plate so he can slide. The catcher wants the runner to slide because he doesn't want to get hurt. Now, if the ball is coming from the left, the catcher can cheat a little bit up the corners so that the runner has to slide a lot more around him, giving the catcher more time to get the ball and put the tag on him. Or the runner could go around him and not catch home plate.

A strike-'em-out, throw-'em-out: the catcher pops up, his arm cocked with the ball at his ear.

On a pitch that gets away or on a pop-up, the catcher takes off his mask, locates the ball, and then throws his mask in the opposite direction so that he doesn't stumble over it.

Turning the Double Play

The most important thing about turning the double play is getting the first out. This is something a lot of players tend to forget. It happens in the big leagues. Somebody tries to throw the ball before he has it in his glove. Or he tries to get the two outs and hurries it and

How Many Outs?

Nothing is more important in the field than knowing how many
outs there are in the inning. The players need to know how
many are on base, but they can see that. They have to know
how many outs there are to correctly assess and play any situation. Nobody wants to repeat the famous Manny Ramirez error
when he tossed the ball to a fan in the stands after catching a fly
ball for the second out. Trouble was, there were men on base.

Tell your players to always remember, or find out, "how many
outs?" And if they know, to waggle their fingers and let all their
teammates know, too. Who knows which one may be thinking of
a girlfriend, or something else.

throws it over the other guy's head. Now instead of getting two outs
he gets no outs. The most important thing is to get the first out. If
you don't get the double play, at least you get the lead runner. That's
very important.

Now let's talk about young kids. The most important thing for
the guy taking the throw at second is to get the ball and take a step
off the base and then throw to first—make sure of the first out and
throw to first.

There are different ways to do that.

Say the second baseman gets the ball from the shortstop. He goes
over to the base, steps with his right foot on the base as he's catching
it, steps off the base, takes a crow hop, and throws to first base—
stepping over the bag and toward the pitcher's mound. He doesn't
want to throw it directly over to first because most younger kids
don't slide, so he's going to need to get a better angle.

The shortstop takes the ball from the second baseman, steps on
the bag with his right foot, steps through the base, takes a crow
hop, and throws to first. It's simple. Try to make it simple for the
younger kids.

Younger kids may not turn a double play all season. It's pretty
hard when they're little, partly because the ball is usually not hit

The shortstop fields the ball and throws to the second baseman, who is ready to fire to first and finish a 6-4-3 double play.

hard enough. But they might get a close one. They'll go home and say, "Grandpa, you should have seen it. We almost turned a double play." That's enough that they're proud of a well-executed play. They'll certainly get a lot of joy out of it.

If the second baseman is getting the ball from third, he straddles the base, catches the ball, touches the bag with his right foot, steps off, and throws. It's the same thing. You don't want to make it too technical. Practice will make the kids good at it.

If the first baseman fields the ball along the line that the runner is taking to first, then the shortstop taking the throw sets up inside the base so he is taking it out of the runner's path. He steps on the base with his left foot, and then throws to first. The pitcher should be covering.

Pitchers

In the first part of pitchers' fielding practice (PFP), the coach hits the ball to first and the pitcher gets over to cover the base. In the next part, the double-play ball is hit back to the pitcher and he throws to the shortstop covering second, who throws it on to first. Next, the double-play ball is hit to second and the pitcher has to cover first base for the throw from the shortstop at second base.

Pop-Ups

Like fly balls, the only way players get a good feel for catching pop-ups is to practice catching them. There's no secret, no magic pill. They can catch balls just thrown into the air by a buddy, which gives them a good sense of the idea. But a batted ball does behave a little differently because the spin imparted by the bat is different, so practice with a fungo helps kids understand the skill even better.

Wind is also a factor, and we'll talk about that in the outfield section later in this chapter. (Don't let players skip learning about the outfield just because they expect to play infield. To be ballplayers, they need to know as much about the game as they can; they need to know what everybody else on the team knows.)

Rundowns

The number one rule on rundowns is always run the guy back to the base he came from. Teach your fielders to hold the ball in their throwing hand and run the player back *as hard as they can* until he commits (or until he's so close he has no choice), then throw it. I like to run them back hard, because when they try to stop, they are usually off-balance and can't stop and start.

Players should be backing each other up in the rundown, one after the other, and get out of the way once they've released the ball.

Outfield

Catching a fly ball in the outfield just takes practice and more practice. Nothing else will prepare players to be able to track the course of the ball. After a while, they'll wonder why they found it hard at all. But there are a few cardinal rules.

In a well-executed rundown, the fielder holds the ball high in his throwing hand and chases the runner back, eventually throwing to the defensive player covering the base to finish the play.

The first and foremost rule is always be ready. In the outfield, it can get boring and then, all of a sudden, a ball is hit in the alley. It is imperative that outfielders get that good jump. Their first three steps should be a sprint. They must get themselves moving, then start to look up.

They should use two hands. I've talked about the "TV effect," and here again, one-handed catches are for Andruw Jones, not the beginning or intermediate ballplayer.

The players' first three steps when a ball is hit over their head should be like they're running to second base. They should not drift under the ball. I am a stickler on guys not drifting for balls. If they turn and go, their first three steps should get them to full speed. Then they should look up and find the ball again.

When players are running under the ball, they should try to keep their head even and relatively still. Look at a guy like center fielder Torii Hunter of the Los Angeles Angels of Anaheim, and see how he flies after a ball; he runs, but his head stays constant.

The outfielders should always get to the fence. If they can get to the fence and come back in, it's a lot easier then drifting, drifting, and all of a sudden, oops, the ball is over their head.

They should charge ground balls that are hit to them and get them back into the infield. Outfielders should never hold the ball for more than the time it takes to get it out of their glove. They should field it as an infielder would—with both hands.

On ground balls with runners on base, outfielders have to come up throwing.

If there's nobody on base they can get down on one knee to block the ball, but if there's a runner, they have to catch the ball on the run. If the fielder is right-handed, his left foot has to be out. His left side has to be all together, and he should gather the ball on the left side of his foot and come up throwing in one smooth motion.

With the bases empty, outfielders should get down on the ball like an infielder just to make sure the ball doesn't go by them. Whenever the ball is hit, they should back up their teammates on every play in case the ball gets by them. Nasty bounces in uneven outfields have been known to happen.

Have you watched games where the wind is blowing out? Pitchers may think it's a nightmare, but it's something outfielders have to keep in mind too. I have told my guys, "Don't forget to check the wind" so many times it's become a joke, a cliché with them. They make fun of me.

How do players check the wind? They pick up some grass, and they throw it up and they check it. They do it every inning, because the wind can change direction around the field pretty dramatically in the course of a few minutes.

If the wind is blowing out, it's not only good for the outfielders to check it, but the infielders have to check it, too. Because if the wind is blowing out and a pop-up is hit to short, or around short, and the shortstop is running around a little bit, the outfielder knows that ball is going to carry to him. On the other hand, if it's blowing in, and the ball is hit to medium left field, the shortstop is going out, but he's got to know that maybe the ball is coming back toward the dirt, toward the infield.

Drills

If you're just starting out the season in spring, a word of caution. When you first start workouts you should gradually get into it. Don't start the players throwing hard right off the bat. It's a long season for most of the kids, and you want to save their arms. A lot of people might say, "Well, if he's not throwing hard, he's not getting a good read." But players should build their arm strength up all the time. It's important to go easy at first.

Defensive work should have just as much a place as batting practice. Take infield/outfield every practice. Make sure people can hit their cutoffs. Then go over bunt situations. I believe that high school kids should know how to hit cutoff men, know where they should be in a cutoff situation; they should be able to do bunt plays; pitchers should know their assignments. You should keep going over this, at least once a week to refresh people's memories. This way it stays in their heads, and they know what to do when the situation comes up in a game.

You can use a fungo bat, the Lite-Flight Machine, or a pitching machine; it doesn't matter. (Some Little League–weight aluminum bats may work just as well as a fungo bat.)

A good outfielder gets under the ball, makes the catch with two hands, takes a crow hop, and, with full extension of his throwing arm, is ready to fire the ball in to the cutoff man.

Infield: Modified Basics

If you want to get a lot of ground balls in, have two guys hitting fungoes—one to the right side and one to the left.

First, have them hit straight at the fielders; then go to their left and then their right, back and forth, backhands, forehands.

Then, in our camps, we'll have the third basemen go across for double plays from third to second. And we'll have a short man at first, a first baseman playing between first and second base. What we're doing here is having the third baseman get rid of the ball nice and smooth to second and the second baseman making the transition to throw the ball to first. He doesn't have to throw it all the way over to first, because then you're wearing his arm out.

While I'm doing that, another guy is hitting fungoes to the shortstop, who is throwing over to first base, independently. After we do a few of those, we work short-to-second double plays and second-to-short double plays. We take the other first baseman away here, the guy in the middle, and make the keystone guys throw a little longer, make them complete the double play. But we haven't worn them out.

The third basemen are now working with the other fungo guy, and he's hitting them short ground balls they have to field barehanded, just coming up, but not throwing it over. Then, after we're finished with the keystone pairs, we let the third basemen throw it over to first. Then we work with the first basemen going to second.

Finally, we go around the horn the right way, all the way to first.

We get a lot of work in that way in a short amount of time. And everybody is busy. Meanwhile, the outfielders are taking fly balls, learning to go back on the ball.

Infield: Pop-Ups

Have a coach and a player stand face-to-face. The player is set as if he is ready to field the ball. The coach yells, "go," and the player breaks, runs five or six steps, and catches the ball over his shoulder, which improves a feel for the catch, or "soft hands."

Outfield: Fly Balls with Runners

To drill for getting under fly balls with men on, we'll have a contest between a team in right field and a team in left field. Place a large target at different spots on the infield where an outfielder makes a throw—we use the L-shaped screen batting practice is pitched from—and award one point for hitting the target and five points for hitting a tighter defined part of that target, a bull's-eye.

Infield/Outfield: Cutoffs and Relays

I talked about practicing relays and cutoffs at length, so I won't belabor the point again. It's just something you have to practice. A run is a run. And you often lose by a run. It would be great if your pitcher struck everybody out, but even if he gets all his outs that way, the way you lose is when somebody "gets hold of one." The way you win is that the other team doesn't score more runs on that "one" than they should.

The goal of relay drills is to teach the outfield guys to make a good, proper cutoff throw and to teach the infield guys how to maneuver to take the cutoff and make the throw into the infield (depending on how the throw comes in to them). The cutoff men need to learn to always make throws from the glove side, so they have to learn to move so that they can do this.

Three-Man Relay Drill

We teach the rookies, our younger guys, the three-man relay. Basically, the coach is just going to hit the ball to the different outfielders, and they throw to a cutoff man, the shortstop or second baseman, and he throws to second, third, or home. Generally, the

Setting up for the fly-ball contest

shortstop takes throws from left and center field, and the second baseman from right field. The opposite keystone player should be covering second (second base is the keystone in old-time sportswriters' parlance; the shortstop and second baseman operate around the keystone, the game's usual scoring position).

Four-Man Relay Drill

You should use four men in a relay when a ball is hit deep into a corner or alley, and you may have to employ a double cutoff to get the ball into the infield in an out situation. This is more for older kids, because generally the younger kids aren't going to hit the ball far enough for it to be necessary.

The coach hits the ball so the left fielder has to chase it into the deep left corner; then the shortstop comes out about halfway and the second baseman has to come over to provide what I call a "soft behind," five to six feet behind. If the throw from the left fielder is bad and gets by the shortstop cutoff, the second cutoff, the second baseman, can clean it up and make the throw into the infield or home.

In all cases, the first baseman needs to be moving wherever he may be needed, and it's probably not first. Nobody there is likely to count just now. He may need to cover second, he may need to back up throws, but he has to be involved. This is a good drill to get him used to the idea.

It's also a good drill for pitchers to teach them their backup responsibilities. Pitchers have two key spots in all these situations, and they are both to stop runs. If a pitcher doesn't run way back behind third base, I mean way back, by the dugout, on any possible play at third, he is only hurting himself. Any ball that gets out of play there means at least one run. By the same token, he needs to be behind the plate if the play could be there.

The first baseman needs to be aware in each situation where he can be of the most use. He doesn't want to be the player gazing around when the winning run is scored on an errant throw. Trust me, there are errant throws in baseball.

On a double cutoff from the right field corner, it is the second baseman who gets halfway out and the first baseman who provides the "soft behind." If a first baseman is unsure on tough outfield situations, he should at least position himself in the middle of the infield where he can react.

Situation Drills

We split up into two teams: one is running and one is fielding. We'll have a fungo hitter and a man on first. The first order of business is a double play. We'll hit a ball in the alley; now there's a guy running and they have to set up their relays. It's something that coaches should do all the time to make sure everybody knows what he's doing. We do it at the college level because even though the players know the routine they still have to practice it to make it perfect every time.

If you practice situations enough, your players will think that's all they do. But they'll know baseball, they'll play baseball right, and if they really can pitch and hit, the breaks will seem to take care of themselves.

Education

One aspect of sports that I stress to the students at my camps and my college players is something that I was never told about: the importance of academics. I tell the kids from day one of my camps that they should get into a routine with their studies.

There's nothing worse for a coach then telling a player and his parents that he doesn't qualify for a scholarship because his grades aren't good enough. I learned this lesson the hard way. I had 40 scholarship offers, but I had to go to summer school to qualify to play my freshman year.

Let's say a player is a good left-handed pitcher and I think he can pitch for me. The first thing I'm going to ask is, "What's your GPA and your SAT score?" If he's got a 2.0 and 800 on his college boards, I can't even think about him. I have to go to the next guy because I know he's not going to get accepted into the school. There are other schools where he can go to play ball, but maybe not the school of his choice. And I've seen that happen. That's why it's very important to have a good education, and it's very important to start early.

A good work ethic is key. I like to use my wife and daughter as examples. Beginning when our daughter was in the first grade, my wife made sure that when she got home from school, she would always do her homework while she was still in the same frame of mind—when she wasn't tired. Because what happens? Kids come home, they change their clothes, they go outside for a little while, they eat, and then they get tired. They don't want to do anything after dinner. So I recommend to my players that they do their homework early, while they're still going, when they haven't slowed down yet. I think if players develop that habit, just like they develop a habit of going to play ball, they'll really enjoy the dividends.

Parents have their part. If parents would spend half the time and money on tutoring their children as they spend on the fees, the camps, the equipment, the trips, and the showcases, they would be better for it in the end.

I tell the kids in the summer, "You guys are getting a big advantage here in this camp. I'm not talking about what you are going to learn about baseball. The most important lesson you can take away is just how important school is. That's your advantage: to learn that lesson. So that someday, you can say, 'Hey, Coach Scala told me about this a long time ago, and now it's here. Boy, am I glad I listened to him on that.'"

If I can help a kid learn that lesson, that's a successful camp to me, too.

10
Play Smart

I took your 'bunny' pitch *down*," shouts the happy camper to the youthful pitcher, as he rounds first base after stroking a sharp line drive to left field. The sky is beautiful with just a few whispery horsetails of clouds in a brilliant blue. The kids are all laughing, poking fun at each other, behaving the way kids do when they're playing a game they love in the height of a glorious summer afternoon. They've just spent a week at school, except it was baseball school, and dreary fall classes seem like months away. They've learned a lot in my baseball camp, though, and on this day, the last day, their confidence in practicing their newfound skills bubbles over into the familiar schoolyard razzing. The last day's morning session of my camps is filled with a Home Run Derby, a Gold Glove contest, and an accurate throw contest. The contests are a reward for the guys' hard work all week and are to get them ready for the championship games to be played in the afternoon session.

"Hey, Kevin, play short and pay attention!" yells instructor Steve Malvagna (who played for me at Adelphi and signed with the New York Mets).

"Hey Kevin, play short and shush!" yells the diminutive 13-year-old third-base coach.

"I can do both!" yells back the shortstop.

Sometimes the tendency of young minds to wander creeps out, or maybe it is just the exuberance of the day.

"Hey, look at that cloud! It looks like an arrow. It's awesome," says a kid standing at first after drilling a shot to left center. Then everybody's attention is briefly taken by a dust devil, a small swirl that looks like a miniature tornado in the dry clay on the infield around second base.

"Let's go, Jake!" Jake is batting. "That's your pitch, Jake!" the kid coaching first base yells, trying to apply a coach's recent comment to him. He's learned the lesson to swing at strikes he can hit.

On the bench, a player is relating a particularly funny story to a teammate, a move he's put over on a One-on-One coach. "I said, 'You gonna take this from a kid born in '94?" More laughter. More confidence. Kids can have fun and learn at the same time. We are not the marines, but we do instill discipline when we need to.

The kids not playing on the field occupy themselves on the bench with a "reaction ball," a multibubbled rubber ball that is unpredictable in its bounces and improves players' fielding, especially of ground balls that take bad hops. Youth league baseball can often be played on some pretty chippy infields. The "reaction ball" also forces concentration and teaches the fielder to keep his hands down, in front of him, and ready. And it's something two kids can play anywhere they won't break anything (though the ball is pretty soft), with or without gloves.

Meanwhile, a heavyset kid, the kid dubbed Manny Ramirez by the campers, who has doubled, is taking off for third.

"Oh my gosh, he's stealing," comes a chorus from the bench. Plenty of laughter, and "I can't believe it!"

"It's the hardest base to steal, too," says another young camper, confident of his lessons.

But that's it for the day. Coach Don McCormack yells, "Pack up your gear!" and the kids get to it, with disappointment—"Ahh, that's all?"—and good sportsmanship.

"Good game, you guys, we all played well," says one young guy, who's picking up on leadership.

"Did anybody on our team strike out?" asks a boy with thick blond hair so long it's sticking around his ears from his cap.

"Hey, Joe, did you strike out?" he yells.

"Yes," Joe sighs. "Again," he emphasizes, but with a tone that says he can work it out. He'll make an adjustment.

As the boys start cleaning up the dugout, mostly gathering gear and the plastic cups they used for ice water from the cooler, they start throwing the water around, first in cups, then in whatever quantity they can find, until a whole thermos is emptied on one ice water–playing kid.

At my camps, we like to let the kids play. We keep them in line and won't tolerate talking when we are teaching a lesson, but kids play. It's what they do. We want this game to be fun for them, not another chore to be endured as the summer slides away.

It's back in the vans then, because we've got to get back to our home field for awards.

Recognition, Praise, and the Family

At our home field, the families have gathered, moms and pops, granddads and grandmothers, the guys' brothers and sisters, cousins, aunts and uncles. It's quite a crowd we get, of parents and family members interested in their children's development. We're lucky because most of the folks who send their kids to our camps are pretty involved in the first place.

All the kids show improvement, and most of the time it's pretty tough to pick our All-Stars and our MVPs, but some kids are just more talented, and they need that recognition. We recognize the "hardest worker" and the "most improved" player, too. These awards are very dear to me. They show hard work and dedication for the week in all aspects of the camp.

The parents enjoy the ceremony that recognizes that all the kids have worked hard and become better ballplayers. The kids cheer each other, and they know who plays a little bit better. It would be odd not to recognize it. One of the great things about my camp and baseball in general is the camaraderie that players establish. We have kids from Brooklyn, Queens, Long Island, New Jersey, and even as far as Pennsylvania. They all listen, learn, and respect each other, because of the one constant—the love of baseball.

I tell the kids, "You will remember your friends from baseball forever, because you will do memorable things together. Like win championships." Then I show them my World Series ring. To this day, when I get together with the old Yankees, we share memorable stories that bring us together again. I think the kids get it when I show them "the Ring."

Some leagues these days don't keep score and declare every kid a winner. But there are winners and losers in life, and just because you lose one game doesn't mean you're going to lose the next. In fact, some teams rebound from a series of losses and, maybe even playing above their heads, win some games they're not expected to. This works in the majors, too. Look at all the wild-card teams that have won the World Series. That's one of the most important life lessons baseball teaches that you won't find in other sports. There's always tomorrow, the next game, next year, when things change and losing becomes winning. To quote the late, great satirist George Carlin, there's no "sudden death" in baseball, only "extra innings."

So when I put a cap to the end of a week in camp, with medals for everybody, awards for many, and recognition for a job well done, it seems fitting. The kids like it, and that's an important thing.

I also get a chance to thank the parents for bringing their kids to camp, encouraging them to get involved in team sports and stay active in their children's lives. I thank them for letting me and my staff teach the kids one-on-one, because to see the kids improve gives us as much pleasure as it does them.

Moving On to High School

Our older kids are getting ready to cross into that great leveler—high school. That's what we're trying to get the guys ready for, the real competition. At this level, it's no longer a given that everybody plays. They may not even make the team, especially at the big high schools that can have a couple hundred kids try out.

But if they do make it, there's a lot to look forward to, because at the high school level, they begin to do some of the more involved things you see in the pros, they get to play with more tools. Strategy really begins to come into play.

Some Basic Game Strategy: Defense

Before the game starts—and I'd recommend this to the high school guys, maybe not so much for younger kids—be sure you know who the best hitters are on the other team. Call other coaches or players who have played them before. Maybe you should know their averages, if they're available. In college, we know the statistics on every team we play.

I count four major things, and in this order: batting average; runs batted in; who's hot right now; and who runs, who is likely to steal bases. Also at my disposal is how they hit against right-handed and left-handed pitchers. This information is especially helpful when situations develop.

Let's say there are runners at second and third base, one or two outs, and it's a close game. The leadoff hitter is coming up, and he's hitting .365. The next hitter is hitting .265. Well, I'm going to tell our guys to pitch away from the .365 guy, and we're going to go after the .265 guy. I'm going to go with the percentages.

Let's say, now, that there's a runner on first base and I have a star next to his name on the scorecard. He's been successful on 14 of 16 attempted steals. We're going to keep that guy close. We're going to make sure we throw over. When we do our pickoffs, we make sure we get a fast one over, a quick move, not a routine move. We're going to hold the ball on him: the pitcher comes set and just waits longer than usual, until the batter calls time-out. That helps freeze the runner's legs. We're trying to keep him out of his rhythm to steal.

Some Basic Game Strategy: Offense

On the offensive side, sometimes I like to bunt. I don't like to bunt early in the game; I like to let my guys swing. But if we're not scoring runs, then we're going to have to bunt a little bit more. Maybe you have to bunt to move runners over.

Maybe someone's not swinging the bat well, even though he's a good hitter. Sometimes I can get his bat going by getting him swinging on a hit-and-run in a certain situation (the runner steals and the batter has to put his bat on the ball).

A hit-and-run can accomplish a couple of things: you can maybe stay out of the double play with the runner moving early; the runner may be able to take an extra base on a single; the ball may go through the hole left by the infielder going over to cover second base. If the ball goes through where the shortstop was, the hitter has a single instead of a double-play grounder. His confidence gets a boost, and maybe so does his bat.

Playing Smart Baseball

If there is a cardinal rule to winning baseball it's this: play smart. That goes both offensively and defensively.

We teach signs in our camps to the kids 10 and older. But we keep it simple. Steal and bunt. It's part of our job of "keeping it simple" and teaching the proper way to play through repetition.

Signs for stealing, delayed steals, hit-and-runs, bunts for hits, sacrifices, and, of course, for pitching, are more advanced stuff. We'd rather the kids know how to do all those things first. But signs become important in high school ball because the players are supposed to know now how to execute those plays.

Lost Chances

Playing smart, then, means your players know all your team's signs. Playing smart means making sure they execute properly, do everything the right way. If they get the sign for a delayed steal, make sure they delay. If you have a hit-and-run on, make sure they get the sign. You don't want a player to leave your runner out to dry by taking a pitch when he should be trying to get his bat on the ball whatever or wherever it is. The runner shouldn't make the hitter swing at something he doesn't like because he missed the sign to go with the pitch.

It's very important for your players to get the signs. You can only do some things at certain times, so if they miss the opportunity, you'll never get it again. That opportunity is lost when a player misses the sign.

Anticipation

On defense, playing smart is something we've talked about a lot: players must know the situation. It's very important.

Let's say there's a man on third base. Whatever position someone is playing, he should know ahead of time where he wants to go with the ball if it's hit or thrown to him. He should anticipate each opportunity, each situation. If the ball is hit right to the third baseman, he's got to get the guy at home. If it's hit to his left, then he goes to first base, or second base if it's a first and third situation. But he has to know the situation before it comes.

If it's a sacrifice fly, players must know where they're supposed to be for cutoffs or relays. If they're in the outfield, they should know their cutoff man, and throw it there. If there's no play for the runner at home, they should know where to throw it in the next case. The catcher should be guiding the team, but the players should not expect to wait for last-minute help. They should know where to throw.

No fielder should make needless throws. Many errors come from throws that shouldn't have been made in the first place.

Smart Adjustments

At all levels, players should make adjustments for powerful hitters, or for guys who like to pull the ball.

As we were putting this book together, we had such a situation at Adelphi. We were playing the University of Bridgeport. There was one little guy I noticed hitting in the batting cage before the game. He was hitting the ball pretty well, taking good cuts. When he came up to the plate later, a lot of my guys, noticing that he wasn't very big, were playing him too shallow. I moved them back. He hit the ball to the warning track, but we caught it. That little guy had more than a little pop in his bat.

How do you know a kid can hit in Little League, when you've never seen him or his team before?

You watch his stance at the plate. You watch him in the field, how he conducts himself. You can tell he's a player. Maybe you watch him take his first cut. You say, "This kid's got a good swing." So you play him back a little bit. Move your guys back. Tell them, "Be ready, because if this kid connects, he's going to hit the ball pretty good."

Planning a Pitching Strategy

Brian Corbo handles pitching and pitching development for me at Adelphi. He goes over scouting reports on opposing teams, their hitters, what the hitters' tendencies may be, and the strategies we may use against them. We have charts of our conference opponents from previous years, and we can see where they've hit the ball and what the pitch sequence was. We also try to do an analysis of the five past games the team has played from the more limited league data we get. It tells where the ball was hit and whether it was a ground ball, for instance, but it doesn't say, of course, what pitches the hitter saw. Obviously, on the guys we've played against for a couple of years, we've got a pretty good grasp on what kind of hitters they are, and Brian can develop a plan to pitch against them. He'll go over the plan for the opposing team with the pitcher and catcher before the game, and then he'll also brief the bull pen. Between innings he'll continue to talk with the catcher and pitcher to see how our plan is working out, whether they're seeing something he's not seeing, whether we need to make some adjustments.

"Obviously, we're going with the game plan assuming the pitcher has all his stuff that day," Brian says. "Sometimes he doesn't. Maybe one day, his changeup is not as good as usual, or his breaking ball is not as sharp, then we'll have to adjust.

"I call pitches to a certain extent, but I really like the guys to do it themselves. I'm always there if the catcher wants to make a quick peek over in the dugout and get a sign from me. But if the pitcher is not comfortable with that sign, if they shake it off, that's fine. As long as they have an explanation when they come in. If they felt confident in that pitch, that's fine with me," Brian says.

"My main philosophy with my guys is that, regardless of what I'm teaching them, they have to feel comfortable with what they're doing when they get out to the mound. I'm not trying to make anybody robotic, and concerned with 'what I say goes.' "

Brian is a smart guy, and I agree with him. The most successful pitchers are guys who develop their own routines that they're comfortable with. We emphasize routine from day one, and we adjust their pitching routine from there.

Strategies to Get Guys Out

For a dead-pull hitter, Brian says, "You're going to stay away from a lot of hard stuff on the inner half, because that's what they're looking to do—just yank everything. If you're going to throw in, it's going to be up on their hands to tie them up. But you don't want to leave it on the inner half.

"You're going to throw a lot of breaking balls away because a pull hitter is just going to roll his hands and hit it basically into the ground. Or you'll see some fly balls the opposite way because they're out in front of the pitch, swinging early."

You want to keep the ball out of a pull-hitter's hitting zone, which is middle of the plate to inside plate. You can pitch them tight, on the hands, as long as the ball doesn't stray a little more to the middle of the plate. Generally speaking, when you get to the college level, you'll need to stay out of the middle of the plate, because these guys can hit fastballs.

"We don't throw pitches down the middle in bull pen sessions. I tell the guys, 'If you can't throw the ball down the middle, you might as well find another sport.' It just isn't going to cut it at the college level," Brian says.

But you can get too cute, too. Remember that adage from Ray Miller: "Work fast. Change speeds. Throw strikes."

For a first-ball hitter, guys that swing at the first pitch 9 times out of 10, we're not giving them anything on that first pitch anywhere in the strike zone where they can handle it. We're pitching them to swing at a ball in the dirt outside, or up and away, nothing that's really going to be a strike.

For a good-average hitter, a guy who can generally handle most pitches, the scouting report really helps. "Hopefully, it can tell you what pitch gets him out, in what sequence," Brian says.

You'd want the pitcher to throw more breaking balls earlier in the count (remember we're talking about pitchers who are at least sophomores or juniors in high school for curves and sliders; younger kids can use a changeup). Then more fastballs later in the count, which is what we call pitching backward. A lot of good-hitting kids are pretty aggressive at the plate and like the fastball, so we're not going to give it to them early in the count.

We'll give them a curveball, and then come back with the fastball. Not something they can handle, but something outside or in on the hands. They may be looking for a fastball, but we want to give them something they're not going to be able to handle.

These guys are the tough outs. We're not really trying so much to outthink him, as to not give him the pitch he wants early in the count, and try to get ahead in the count. If we're ahead, the hitter has to hit our pitch rather than his pitch, or something fat and easy. If it's a pitcher's count, the batter may get a pitch he can handle, but he should be in a more defensive mode, where he's not going to get as good a bat on it.

Pitcher Counts

Every pitcher is different. They all have a slightly different out pitch, a pitch they go to. Some guys can throw it by anybody. But they all have to have command of that pitch. What a pitcher throws best affects how you would approach each batter.

Generally, the first time through the order, we'll throw mostly fastballs at the lineup to see whether they can handle it. If they show that they can, well, they'll probably be seeing some breaking stuff next time around. Pitching backward means using the off-speed stuff to set up the fastball down in the zone, on the hands, or outside the zone, to see if we can get them to chase it. After a diet of slow stuff, some guys' eyes just light up when they see that fastball at their shoulders, where it's tough to do much of anything constructive.

"Another X-factor is the umpire," Brian says. "Early in the game, I'm looking to see where the umpire's strike zone is. I always tell my catchers, 'When we're setting up for the outside fastball, see how much you can get. Get out there as far as you can.' If the ump's giving it to us out there, then we're going to sit out there until he stops. We want to see if we can expand the strike zone."

If the umpire is calling it tight, then we're going to have to change the hitter's eye level. That means we'll throw it low and away, maybe, and then up and inside. Changing where the ball is coming from works on the hitter the same way changing speeds does. It puts some doubt in his mind about what is coming next. The hitter has less than a second to react to a pitched ball, so any doubt helps the pitcher.

It's a Small Baseball World

Life can sure throw you a lot of curveballs. There seem to be some remarkable coincidences along the way for everybody. Let me tell you about one that's worked out real well for me.

I first met Bobby Malvagna when we both played for St. John's University. I was a senior when he came up as a freshman on scholarship. He says he got the scholarship when the college coach came to one of his high school games on Staten Island to look at another player, and Bobby just happened to have a great game as shortstop that day. You can maybe take him at his word, but he's a self-deprecating man by nature.

We kept in touch a little bit over the years, but we went separate ways. I went on to play in the pros and ended up coaching and scouting. Bobby became a commodities broker at the New York Mercantile Exchange. They're the guys who start out on the trading floor, shouting and quickly buying and selling future contracts on commodities like oil, corn, and pork bellies. That's a pretty intense way of life, but he stayed at it for 20 years, past the endurance of most guys. He, of course, raised his three boys to be ballplayers, too, one of whom was signed by the New York Mets.

Like I said, we kept in touch, but there were a lot of gaps, until we both ended up coaching in the same high school league. So we met up again, and baseball was the reason why. Then a year or so later, I was offered the Adelphi job as coach of the Panthers' pretty ailing baseball team. Bobby, it turned out, was already there. Well, I know a lot about Bobby's approach and skill set, so I made him my associate coach. He's spent half his life in the high-pressure Mercantile Exchange, but here he is coaching baseball for a living, just like I've always been doing.

Bobby is also my assistant at the One-on-One Baseball camps.

"I think it's rewarding that at the end of the week, two weeks, you have a kid who, on Monday, didn't know how to throw the ball, didn't know how to grip the ball, didn't know how to catch a ball, at the end knows how to do those things," Bobby says. "He knows something about the game, has a sense of the game. For me, it's just like a teacher in school. They teach the kids in history, spelling, and English. In my case, I teach the game of baseball. For me, that's the rewarding part."

What College Scouts Are Looking For

I'm going to let Bobby speak to some of the things that we at Adelphi University look for in high school kids that encourage us to recruit them for our college team. These are things that tell us that a kid can succeed at the next level, and for that reason, things that coaches of younger players should be laying the foundation for with their kids.

Pitchers

What are we looking for from kids on the mound?

"First-pitch strikes is a big thing when we go to recruit guys," Bobby says. "When we look at pitchers, we look at how many strikes they throw and then take it even further and see how many were first-pitch strikes. Is he starting 0-and-1? Or 1-and-0? The successful guys are going to be up throwing first-pitch strikes around 60 to 65 percent of the time. A guy that's throwing 25, 28 percent strikes is going to be in trouble an awful lot. That's one of our recruiting tools we use to keep track of the guys we want to bring into our program."

Some kids may be a little rough around the edges in high school, but a good scout can find good things in a shaky outing.

"There's a certain saying, 'You can't teach 90 [miles per hour].' But a guy that's 91 may be a little erratic, and we can see that maybe there's a small mechanical flaw, maybe his release point is off. That's something that as a coaching staff you can work through or work out of. But like in basketball, you can't teach 6′7″, you can't teach 92," he says.

Hitters

What are we looking for from kids at the plate?

"In a hitter, I look for bat speed, number one," Bobby says.

"I also look for, believe it or not, the sound of the ball coming off the bat, especially with the wood bat. You can tell that a guy hits the ball well, he's not hitting the ball off the handle, he's not hitting off the end of the bat, he's hitting it right on the sweet spot. It makes a little bit of a different sound. You get a trained ear so that you can know what to look for in a hitter.

"Bat speed is key. You want to see a guy who hits it out in front, who swings and is balanced. He's not falling all over the place, his feet aren't all over the place. There are certain nuances that a good hitter has that we look for," Bobby says. "Some guys are naturals. They're always hitting the ball hard."

But again, the box score can lie. A scout has to actually see the ballplayers in action.

"We don't have to have a guy go four-for-four every time we watch him," Bobby says. "Those 'four-for-fours' may be little dinkers here and there, while the guy who goes 'zero-for-four' but hits four fly balls to the warning track, or hits three good, hard line drives, that's something to take into consideration—how the ball comes off his bat."

Don McCormack

Don McCormack spent *21 years in the Philadelphia Phillies organization, including 10 years as a catcher. He came up to the big leagues in 1980 and 1981, and then spent time with the Cubs and Tigers organizations. He returned to the Phillies as the organization's catching coordinator and helped develop five major-league catchers: Mike Lieberthal, Todd Pratt, Johnny Estrada, Gary Bennett, and Bobby Estalella. He spent three years managing the independent minor-league Long Island Ducks for owner Buddy Harrelson. Don lives in the Tampa Bay area, but he has given private lessons and camps in the New York area in the summer when he wasn't otherwise working for a professional club. His son was drafted out of high school in Tarpon Springs, Florida, and played for Milwaukee for a couple years.*

Following is his advice for parents, players, and coaches.

Let's say you're the parent of a talented child who has a real desire to play baseball and move on to the next level. Should you hire an individual coach or seek out special instruction?

Yes, if you get the right person. Usually, you're going to go with somebody with pretty much more experience than maybe a high school coach can teach them. It makes a big difference. It really, really does. I've got maybe 70 kids between boys and girls—and they're getting all this knowledge that I've learned from all these other guys who've taught me over the last 30 years.

How much good direction can you get from amateur coaches? Depending on some of your high schools, the direction gets worse.

What's individual coaching like?

I have had a number of kids for two, three, four years. A lot of the kids I have play for travel leagues, and they come back for tune-ups, at the end of summer as league play winds up, in the winter, before spring practice. You know baseball, everybody struggles. And they'll come back to see, "What's going on with this?"

For instance, I had one kid who's a really good player, but all of a sudden, he's standing up there and he's getting caught too much, he's struggling. I told him, "Stand yourself up, get a better picture of the ball."

He went to Georgia, to East Cobb [a national center of baseball development]. In that area, it's just baseball players for the picking. He went down there, and he couldn't believe how well he was seeing the ball and how well he did.

It was just something simple: "Just put your head a little different; put your eyes in a good position." Little, bitty things.

A lot of times, it's not that high-tech. Something very simple, very easy. Baseball is a lot of repetition. You just learn a very simple way and you keep repeating it.

That's something younger kids don't understand because they get bored so easily. You have to understand: it's just repeat it and repeat it. I tell the kids I teach in New York, "The only difference between you guys and the guys down in Florida is not your abilities, it's just how many more times they do it. They know how to do it a little bit better."

Summer camps are a bigger deal in the North because high school seasons are short and you have to fight the weather. Half the schedule gets rained out. For a kid to come out of there and play somewhere is very fortunate, because for a college or pro scout to come see him play, it's like trying to find a needle in a haystack.

Down South, heaven forbid, if you don't catch a kid pitching one day, you can go back in five days right across the street or something and watch him pitch again. There's so much opportunity.

What about showcases, where some for-profit organizations invite high school players to visit for simulated tryouts and exhibition games in front of scouts?

It's a good idea for some of the kids to go, for instance from up North, who don't get the opportunity to expose themselves that much. I would suggest that they try to put themselves in front of as many pairs of eyes as they can. Because as long as the kid wants to play, there's someplace out there that they can play. But now if they limit themselves to, "Why, I just want to go to St. John's, or I just want to go to Ohio State, or I just want to go to Whatsamatta U.," well, then they limit themselves.

Just in Florida, there are many, many Division I programs, many more junior college programs; there is some place you can play, if you want to go play there. But you have to be willing to leave the nest, in order to go and play. There is someplace for everybody.

A special coach is one thing for a child who wants to be a pitcher, but what about a hitter, or a catcher, or any other position?

I would find a special instructor in that particular area who can get you a good start, and then it's about playing more games. The more games you can play the better off you will be. I would get an instructor first, because it means so much to have a good start. Then you improve your skills, instead of just being another player.

And this certainly goes for young women, as well. My experience has been, those girls that I've taught are wonderful to instruct. They're like sponges, and they apply what they learn so much quicker than the boys do. They put a lot of focus on what they're doing.

I would tell anyone that has someone that's interested in playing to go find a special instructor, because you can see your kids develop so much faster. You go around and you watch these kids play and you know the ones who have been taught and the ones who haven't. It's just getting to a point, I think, where that's what it's coming to. If you actually want your child to progress and have success at the next level, it's the path to take.

If they're struggling in school, what do you do? You go and get a tutor. For whatever subject you need. It's the same way with baseball as with anything else. If you see that they're struggling and they want to have an opportunity at the next level, you can get someone to help. There are plenty of good instructors out there. Plenty.

Conclusion

In writing this book I have retraced my baseball journey. It amazes me what an unexpected turn it took. As a young man in college, I dreamed that my fulfillment in baseball would be "going to the show." However, I realize now that my true fulfillment didn't come from playing baseball but from teaching it.

I always felt comfortable giving tips, or, as I say, "adjustments," to players from Yankees great Goose Gossage to Adelphi's third round draft pick (by the Minnesota Twins) Bobby Lanigan or to my seven-year-old nephew, Joseph Capitelli. I have learned from and listened to many great mentors, some of whom have been mentioned in this book. I didn't do it for monetary gain—I did it for the love of the game. I get a big thrill from teaching kids of all ages and seeing them succeed. When I see a great relay from the outfield, it makes me feel as good as if someone hit a home run. Why? Because we work on drills that tell me the kids are getting it.

I can honestly look my students in the face and say, "I care about your progress and success."

I hope I enlightened you or inspired you to be better coaches. I hope that you put these ideas to good use and make your practices more organized and, most important, make your players have fun and work hard to be fundamentally sound.

I will leave you with this: "Keep it simple" and "perfect practice makes perfect."

Index